The Land We Love

Ian Braybrook

with
Glenn Braybrook

Marilyn Bennet Publishing
100 Brown Street
Castlemaine
Victoria 3450

Copyright © Ian Braybrook 2019

All rights reserved. Without limiting the rights under copyright, no part of this publication may be reproduced, stored or introduced into a retrieval system, or transmitted in any form or by any means (electronic, mechanical, photocopying, recording or otherwise) without the prior written permission of the writer and the publisher.

ISBN: 978 0 9944370 5 1

A catalogue record for this book is available from the National Library of Australia

Cover image:
Eugène Von Guérard, *A view from Mt Franklin towards Mount Kooroocheang and the Pyrenees* c.1864. Purchased 2008 with funds from Philip Bacon AM through the Queensland Art Gallery Foundation.
Collection: Queensland Art Gallery | Gallery of Modern Art, Brisbane.
Photograph: QAGOMA. Used with kind permission.

While the author and publisher have made every reasonable effort to locate, contact and acknowledge copyright owners, any copyright owners who are not properly identified and acknowledged should contact the publisher so that corrections can be made in the next edition.

Design and layout by Level Heading (levelheading.com.au)

Dedication

Dedicated to my late brother, Alan James Braybrook of Tibooburra NSW. He was the quintessential Aussie bushman, loved by all who knew him. His knowledge of the land he loved – the far west of New South Wales – and his respect for the Aboriginal People was inspirational to me. To protect his knowledge of Aboriginal sites he took many secrets with him; most are unlikely to ever be rediscovered.

Acknowledgements

My grateful thanks to Bernard Schultz of Level Heading. His help with research, editing, preparation of the manuscript for printing and general assistance are responsible for the quality presentation of this work.

My thanks to my publisher, Marilyn Bennet, for her continuing help and encouragement. To Auntie Julie McHale for her guidance in Aboriginal matters. Thanks to the late Bill Davies and to Chris Long, descendent of George Vivian, for use of photographs.

I could not have written this story without referring to innumerable written works which extended over many, many years. Thank you all.

Glenn wishes to extend his thanks to Uncle Brien Nelson, John Tully and Gerry Gill. He especially thanks Clive Wilman and David Bannear for their work in confirming his identification of the site of the Forest Creek Monster Meeting.

Aboriginal and Torres Strait Islander Peoples are advised that this book contains the names and images of deceased people.

Disclaimer: Although every effort has been made to check and explore the authenticity of claims and observations made in this publication, the authors and the publisher understand that they may cite material that is in fact incorrect. No resposibility is accepted for such.

Contents

The Land We Love ~ ~ ~ ~ ~ ~ ~ ~ ~ ~ *i*

Foreword ~ ~ ~ ~ ~ ~ ~ ~ ~ ~ ~ ~ ~ *iii*

Part One

The Aboriginal People ~ ~ ~ ~ ~ ~ ~ ~ **5**

Part Two

The Land and its Squatters ~ ~ ~ ~ ~ ~ **21**

Part Three

Gold ~ ~ ~ ~ ~ ~ ~ ~ ~ ~ ~ ~ ~ ~ **71**

Part Four

The Railway ~ ~ ~ ~ ~ ~ ~ ~ ~ ~ ~ **113**

Part Five

Industry and Other Things ~ ~ ~ ~ ~ ~ **131**

Epilogue

Big Changes Come to Town ~ ~ ~ ~ ~ ~ **145**

The Land We Love

We acknowledge Aboriginal people as the traditional custodians of the land and acknowledge and pay respect to them, their Elders past and present.

We are sensitive to the ways, beliefs and customs of Aboriginal people and the protocols that surround them, in line with the Gulanga Good Practice Guide. Variance from this may occur when we take a quotation from other sources; for example, the terms 'natives' or 'blacks' are retained in quotations from contemporaries for authenticity.

The principal focus in our story is on the Dja Dja Wurrung country – ranging approximately from the Pyrenees to a little south of Mount Alexander, the generally accepted country of the original inhabitants.

We do not profess to be anything other than keenly interested locals who have spent a lot of time looking at the past and present of this land; we fancy that we are storytellers. We attempt to convey to our readers what we have learnt over many years. Our sources are many and varied, too numerous to properly recall. We believe that what we relate is accurate, and we are keenly aware of the need to be correct in writing our history.

Much of the information comes from personal experience and, in some cases, items relayed by trusted friends and senior, long-time residents of the area. Where sources are known or recalled, they are acknowledged. As residents of Castlemaine district for many years, our bias probably swings toward the Mount Alexander area.

My son Glenn has contributed much to the text and has added valuable and informative notes. His knowledge of this land is unsurpassed and has been gained over three decades. It far exceeds mine. He has studied

Opposite: Eugène Von Guérard, A view from Mt Franklin towards Mount Kooroocheang and the Pyrenees c.1864. Purchased 2008 with funds from Philip Bacon AM through the Queensland Art Gallery Foundation. Collection: Queensland Art Gallery / Gallery of Modern Art, Brisbane. Photograph: QAGOMA..

in detail the region's history and people. Glenn has traversed, on foot, many hundreds of kilometres of the land from east, west, north and south. He has positively identified many historical sites, including that of the Forest Creek Monster Meeting of 1851. He has accumulated considerable knowledge of the heritage and customs of the local Aboriginal people, plus the location of associated sites, former and remaining. He has also contributed many of the photographs. Some of the pictured localities are not identified in the text and are kept secret for their protection. Similarly treated are the photographs of Aboriginal sites taken by the late Bill Davies, featured in his book *On Country*. Bill's work in this area was outstanding and is invaluable.

We are sympathetic to the original inhabitants of this land and express our regret for the manner in which they were treated far too often. We believe that we Australians are now making a real effort to say 'Sorry'. It is worth remembering that the early atrocities and bad treatment of Aboriginal people were committed by British people, in particular English and Scottish. At that time, brutality and cruelty were customary and were government practice in Britain. The convicts in Australia's early days were accustomed to ill-treatment because it was constantly inflicted upon them; brutality was a reality of life.

Today's Australians are unlike that.

Three events changed the Aboriginal Peoples' ways and their land forever, the invasion by the white people, the discovery of gold and the coming of the railway.

Foreword

Not so long ago, this was a silent land. The only sounds were the birds and the native animals, the wind in the trees and the gurgling water of the pristine streams. As well, there was the occasional chatter of voices from the small families of local people. In the valley nestled beneath the towering mountain, Leanganook, (now Learganook) the voices were of the Liarga-balug clan of the Dja Dja Wurrung. Their valley provided for their every need – an abundance of wallaby and kangaroo, plenty of fish and ample quantities of fresh food from the trees, bush and earth. They wanted for nothing. They owned nothing. The land was the basis of their lives.

Then, one day, it was 28th September 1836, there came another sound – one that the people of the valley had never heard before – the plod of horses' hooves, the rattle of chains, the creaking of wooden wheels, the crack of a whip and loud voices speaking a strange tongue. These sounds heralded the arrival of the white man and the beginning of the end of the way of life that the Aboriginal people had enjoyed for many, many centuries. This would soon be replaced by white men with their sheep, guns and diseases. Soon after, there came more white invaders who turned over the virgin soil and polluted the streams in search of a mysterious golden metal.

These are the stories of how this change came about and how this land changed from a peaceful haven for its inhabitants to a bustling, troubled, sometimes ruined, landscape, filled with a different type of people.

Soon the Aboriginal people's food supply vanished as kangaroos and other native animals were shot and dispersed. Trees and shrubs were cleared away, and with them the native birds and fruits. The roots of the murnong plant, a staple food, were destroyed by the tread of millions of sheep. Hunger forced the Original People to steal the squatters' sheep for food, causing much conflict.

The original inhabitants were soon removed – destroyed is a more accurate word – by greedy, uncaring people who denied them their land, indeed, their very existence. Many who initially survived were later destroyed by white man's diseases and alcohol, killing more than guns ever did.

The white men were now in control.

Part One

The Aboriginal People

In 1837 it was estimated that there were about 6,000 Aboriginal people in the Port Phillip District. They were generally regarded by white people as low on the scale of human development – considered to be in the stone-age of evolution in many respects. For example, the fact that they had not learned how to make pottery from clay, how to extract metal from rock, how to cultivate the soil, or how to develop fruits and grain. They lived on fish, kangaroos, birds, possums, plants and roots – especially murnong.

God only knows how many were killed by white men – poisoning food with arsenic or similar was a common method, according to many reports of the time. Historian Ernest Scott in *A Short History of Australia* wrote that George Augustus Robinson believed this to be a definite cause of the decrease in Aboriginal Peoples' numbers. With regard to population numbers, Scott indicated that the best estimate in 1939 was that there were only about 100 Aboriginal people in all of Victoria.

In Tasmania, as will be mentioned later, the population was almost completely exterminated. Fortunately, George Robinson came onto the scene and he did his utmost to help. He learnt enough of their language to communicate and he really cared. In 1832 he was appointed to remove all those who survived to Flinders Island and in 1835 he did so. There were only 203 survivors of a race which had numbered many thousands when Tasmania was colonised. Most of those relocated to the island soon fretted and died.

It is often claimed that the last full-blooded Tasmanian Aboriginal, Truganini, died in 1860, but this is disputed, considering that at least three

Dja dja Worrung language area and clans. From Ian D Clark.

Aboriginal women survived on Kangaroo Island, Flinders Island and King Island. There is also a continuing presence of Tasmanian Aboriginals.

In 1845, Edward John Eyre wrote:

> 'Could blood answer blood, perhaps for every drop of European's shed by natives, a torrent of theirs, by European hands, would crimson the earth...
>
> 'It is an undeniable fact, that wherever European colonies have been established in Australia, the native races in their neighbourhood are rapidly decreasing, and already in some of the elder settlements, have totally disappeared. It is equally

Images from Major Thomas Mitchell's journal, volume 1.

indisputable that the presence of the white man has been the sole agent in presenting so lamentable an effect; that the evil is still going on, increased a ratio proportional to the number of new settlements formed, or the rapidity with which the settlers overrun new districts. The natural, the inevitable, but the no less melancholy result must be, that in the course of a few years more, if nothing is done to check it, the whole of the Aboriginal tribes of Australia will be swept away from the face of the earth.'

***

Writing in 1788, Colonel David Collins[1] has left us an excellent account of the events that changed the lives of all Aboriginal people of Australia forever. The arrival of white people in Sydney is now, probably correctly, termed an 'Invasion' by the descendants of the original owners.

Following the landing of the crew and passengers of the first fleet, the first actual contact with the original people happened slowly. The Indigenous people had been seen from a distance, they in turn watched these strange people and their equally strange goods and chattels. According to Collins, only two Aboriginal men visited the busy scene in

---

1 Collins, D *An Account of the English Colony in New South Wales* [Volume 1]

the first six weeks following the white people stepping ashore. The two men moved about in curiosity and were each presented with a hatchet before leaving 'well pleased' after about half an hour.

Governor Phillip was a good man and he had issued very strict instructions that no harm be done to any Indigenous person; this appeared to be well adhered to. Some Aboriginal people even helped the crewmen haul in their fishing nets, and were rewarded with generous amounts of fish.

All went well until a group of seamen attempted to land their boat on a small cove, apparently a forbidden area. They were driven off with a shower of stones, the first indication of troubles to come.

Soon after, a party of men from the *Sirius* was preparing a vegetable garden, necessary to supply the settlement with fresh food. A group of sixteen Aboriginal men approached, seized a shovel, spade and pick and ran off with them. One of the fishermen opened fire with his scatter gun, striking a fleeing man in the legs with small shot. He staggered off, seemingly not badly hurt. There was no retaliation.

Some men began stealing the spears, tools and various other items which were of great value to the Aboriginal owners. The purpose was to sell the pieces as curios to the crews of the transport ships, in order to take advantage of the ready sales opportunities in England. These losses had a serious impact on people who depended heavily on these things to provide them with food. There was no nearby store to buy replacements.

There was much upset over an incident involving two convict men foolishly trying to steal things belonging to the Aboriginal people who were in the habit of leaving spears, tools, shields, fishing lines and other items lying about on the rocks and beaches. As the white people were later to learn, Aboriginal people had no sense of personal ownership. Such things were the property of all their people. On seeing the robbery, the Aboriginal people were furious and one man was struck in the back with a spear. His companion ran for his life. The wounded man was stripped of his clothing and left to die. However, he managed to drag himself back to the camp. Although the wound was deep, he eventually recovered. His mate was less fortunate; two days later, his bloodstained clothing was found, but there was no trace of him. It was assumed that he had been murdered.

A short time later, the bodies of two convict workers were found in a cove where they had been working. David Collins wrote: 'they had been pierced with many spears and the head of one beaten to a jelly'. Apparently the two had stolen a canoe for 'which they paid with their lives'.

At about the same time, a number of Aboriginal people were found lying dead in the coves and inlets. It appeared that smallpox was wreaking havoc on people who had no inherited immunity to the disease. It is possible that the Aboriginal people placed the blame for the deaths at the feet of the white men, keeping to the custom of many tribes and clans. Their belief was that nobody died of natural causes. Death was generally considered to be inflicted by another person from another group. Revenge for a death caused many more deaths in a continuing cycle, back and forth.

In the Dja Dja Wurrung country, there was a belief that, sometimes, death or illness was inflicted as punishment by the dreaded Mindye, in that case no retaliation was necessary. On any occasion where a death was not accounted for by human hands, it was believed to be by the Mindye.

In 1788, W Tench wrote:[2]

> 'The unprovoked outrages committed against them by unprincipled individuals amongst us, caused the evil we had experienced.'

Despite the best efforts and intentions of Governor Phillip, killings continued on both sides.

The scene had been set for future relations across Australia.

***

We do not profess to be authorities on Aboriginal people or Aboriginal affairs, we leave that to people who have studied the subject. We write of knowledge gained, mostly by Glenn, over three decades. There is no better authority on the Aboriginals of Central Victoria than John Tully from Dunolly. Indeed, that is the title of his comprehensive book on the subject.[3] Anyone interested in furthering their knowledge of Aboriginal people's heritage and customs in this region should obtain a copy.

John's extensive research has revealed much information, previously unknown, some of which has not pleased everyone. He drew criticism

---

2   Tench, Watkin 1793, *A Complete Account of the Settlement at Port Jackson*.
3   Tully J 2015, *Aborigines of Central Victoria*, Weila Publishing.

A stone depiction of Mindye – bringer of death.

from the Dja Dja Wurrung organisation in Bendigo for his objection to their practice of allowing people to call themselves Dja Dja Wurrung without being actual descendants, and for similarly allowing people to call themselves Uncle, Aunty or Elder.

He has produced highly valued information, which he has willingly shared. Of particular interest is the decline in population of various clans in Central Victoria. Many clans became extinct, some within a few years of the arrival of the white man. Some examples are the Gal Gal Dundidg which, by 1854, had only one survivor and Liarga Balug was reduced to one by 1863, and the Dja Dja Balug clan was extinct by 1841. In his book, John Tully says that the Moonmoon Gundidj, however, has many living descendants. This latter group is of particular interest, given their prominence in Dja Dja Wurrung affairs today.

Notes by Glenn Braybrook

Major Thomas Mitchell was in quite a hurry to return to Sydney. Because of his visit to the Henty's, who were already established at Portland Bay, he worried that one of the ships anchored there might get to Sydney before him. This would almost certainly steal his thunder and downgrade the most exciting discovery of his third expedition: *Australia Felix*.

When he finally reached Sydney, Mitchell's news of that country, and its ready-made sheep runs, ignited what was to become the biggest and most rapid land grab in our history.

The arrival of these intruders signalled devastation for the Aboriginal people already weakened by smallpox, which, in the late 1780s to the 1820s had spread from Sydney and the north, southward through the various clans and tribes. From 1836 onward, to the time the squatters arrived in Dja Dja Wurrung country and took their traditional lands from them, the original people were almost wiped out.

Major Thomas Mitchell (1792–1855)

In Sydney and Yass, overlanding parties were organised by wealthy men to occupy Mitchell's fabulous *Australia Felix*. Within just six months of Mitchell's return, the squatters had begun to move off in groups. For protection three or four different parties would travel together. Their livestock added up to many thousands, mainly sheep, but also numerous cattle and horses.

In 1837, my great-great-grandfather, Abraham Braybrook, a convict servant, was in the very first group to pass close to Mount Alexander and occupy land in central Victoria. Abraham was the group's shoemaker, having been taught the trade while incarcerated in the Portsmouth hulks awaiting transport to New South Wales. He was transported here on the convict ship *Hooghly* in 1834.

At the time of the European invasion, there were fifteen subdivisions of what is now known as the Dja Dja Wurrung, the people who are the traditional occupiers of the Loddon district of central Victoria.

The clan that was local to the Castlemaine–Maldon–Mount Alexander area was the Liarga Balug. According to some interpretations, Liarga translates to mean teeth, and Balug translates to people. This clan may have been named after what surrounded them. The granite formations are said to have looked to them like teeth (perhaps it even referred to the area known today as Dog Rocks on Mount Alexander). However, nobody can be certain how this name came about or its meaning.

The area they occupied is more or less a semi-circle formed by Mount Alexander in the east, with adjoining ranges north to Big Hill and yet more ranges joining it to Mount Tarrangower to the west.

At the time of the white invasion, there were thirty to forty members of the Liarga Balug clan of the Dja Dja Wurrung. In the census of 1841, just 282 members of the entire Dja Dja Wurrung people were left alive. What was the number before the invasion? Some say over a thousand. Nobody can be sure. We do know that the population was deliberately kept low by the Original people. This was done to ensure that the clan would be sustainable and survive in times of drought.

The question is sometimes asked: Who were the first humans to arrive in central Victoria? The answer is, nobody knows. There are suggestions that a smaller, darker race of people arrived first. There is speculation that, much later, the Aboriginal people came here and displaced those who came before them. It is likely, however, that, over thousands of years, bands of people came from the north. What is known, however, is that those very early arrivals found strange trees and an array of unusual animals. Tasmanian devils and Tasmanian tigers (Thylacine), once lived in this area, along with huge kangaroos, wombats the size of small cars, giant emus and other megafauna. There is some suggestion that the arrival of humans caused the extinction of the megafauna, but, again, this is speculation

No single clan laid claim to the whole of this country. Each clan had its own patch of ground and rarely travelled away from the creeks and rivers where plenty of food could be found.

The Aboriginal people had few material possessions. A man had his stone axe, shield and spears and a woman had a digging stick and a dilly bag, which she made from plaited grasses. They were never in one place very long, always on the move, and they took care not to over-fish or over-hunt an area. They constantly moved around their clan area, depending on the seasons which controlled the amount of game and ruled their lives.

The abundance of the yam, which they called murnong, was important. This plant has a small yellow flower, the tuber of which, roasted in oven mounds, was a staple food.

Semi-permanent camps were often made on higher ground above creek and river junctions, where waterholes had formed and the colder air would settle below the camp, helping with warmth. Higher ground also gave better views. It is likely that the shepherds' hut, where the famed Monster Meeting took place at Forest Creek in 1851, was the site for such a camp. This notable site was identified by me, with help from my father, in 2003. There is more about this later.

Sadly, the Aboriginal people were displaced and their waterholes were taken over to supply the sheep and the shepherds.

*Flower of the murnong or yam daisy (*Microseris lanceolata*). Photo by Lorraine Oliver for plantNet (licensed by Creative Commons)*

Waterholes were a feature of our once clean and uncluttered rivers and creeks. The holes were often deep and provided hiding places where fish could survive droughts. Native fish such as Murray cod were found in huge numbers and of large size when this land was first colonised by Europeans.

The Aboriginal People followed rules for the hunting of animals, some were practical, others ritual. Kangaroos, emus, snakes, possums, lizards and even wombats were cooked in clay-lined ovens dug into mounds. The skins were left on and fur was removed later. Murnong root, the staple diet, was treated in the same way.

Something that is hard for us to fathom is that today, some groups of well-meaning folk have planted large numbers of trees in the creek beds. This contributes significantly to water stagnation and causes the streams to flood in times of heavy rain. There may be more awareness of this lately.

The rivers and creeks were severely damaged during the gold rushes. They were polluted and re-routed – changed beyond recognition. Many have never properly recovered.

Marriage among the Aboriginal people was regulated by kinship and traditional laws. One man might have several wives and others, none.

Corroborees had different meanings and reasons, too. Some were performed when a boy was made a man, others were to appease the

A number of wells in a series. It is unusual to find wells so close together. These are all less than 50-60 metres apart indicating a rest spot for travellers.

dreaded Mindye (pronounced min-die), a snake-like creature with a mane like a horse. It was believed to bring death and destruction to the clans. The dreaded Mindye had the power to stretch over huge distances.

I have no doubt that the Aborigines quietly watched Major Mitchell's party pass through this country. In later years, an old Aboriginal woman recalled and described seeing his party move through her clan's country when she was a girl. This unnamed woman became a servant at Bucknall's Rodoborough homestead near present day Carisbrook. On her death she was buried in the homestead graveyard. Her grave was shown to me by historian, John Tully.

More about Major Mitchell's Mt Alexander

I have often visited Mitchell's campsites in Dja Dja Wurrung country. Finding the precise spots where he camped took quite a while and many trips back and forth to the different places mentioned in his writings and journals.

During their return journey to Sydney, Mitchell's party visited the area where the 'friendly mountain', which he had first spied from the Grampians, was located. Mitchell said this mountain seemed to be calling him from afar. The Aboriginal people knew this mountain by many names, but the one that they mostly used is probably Leanganook. However in the present day it is often called Learganook by the Dja Dja Wurrung people.

Mitchell's party moved down the rise now known as McKenzie's Hill, roughly along what is now Ray Street in Castlemaine and crossed Barkers Creek near the railway bridge in Forest Street. From there, his party crossed the later site of Mostyn Street, passed the area where the police station is now, climbed to Kalimna Park, and down the valley where a prominent pine plantation now stands. The group camped in a spot which still has waterholes, and had, until forty years ago, tree ferns and remnant plants from the days before mining denuded the native forest.

Mitchell wrote on the 28th of September:

> 'The steep banks beyond the river [the Loddon at Newstead] consisted of clay-slate having under it a conglomerate containing fragments of quartz cemented by compact haematite.
>
> 'The day was hot and we killed several large snakes of the species eaten by the natives. I observed that our guides looked at the colour of the belly when in any doubt about the sort they preferred; these were white-bellied, whereas the belly of a very fierce one with a large head, of which Piper [an Aboriginal guide] and the others seemed much afraid, was yellow. On cutting this snake open two young quails were found within: one of them not being quite dead. The country we crossed during the early part of the day was at least as fine as that we had left. We passed alternately through strips of forest and over open flats well watered, the streams flowing southward [Muckleford Creek]; and at nine miles we crossed a large stream also flowing in that direction [Barkers Creek about 400 metres from the junction with Forest Creek]: all these being evidently tributaries to that on which we had been encamped [the Loddon at Newstead the night before]. Beyond the greater stream, where we last crossed it, the country presented more of the mountain character, but good strong grass grew among the trees, which consisted of box and lofty bluegum. After making out upwards of eleven miles, we encamped in a valley where water lodged in holes and where we found also abundance of grass.'

This refers to the area that I described earlier as still in pristine condition when I first visited it about forty years ago.

Mitchell continued:

> 'We were fast approaching those summits which had guided me in my route from Mount Cole, then more than fifty miles behind us. Like that mountain these heights also belonged

Top: Major Mitchell's campsite near the overpass of the Calder freeway where it crosses the old highway at Faraday.
Bottom: The cairn at the summit of Mount Alexander from where Mitchell took his readings in 1836.

to a lofty range, and like it were beside a very low part of it, through which I hoped to effect a passage. Leaving the party to encamp I proceeded forward in search of the hill [Mount Alexander] I had so long seen before me, and I found that the hills immediately beyond our camp were part of the dividing range and broken into deep ravines on the eastern side.'

This area is now part of the Diggings National Park at Golden Point, adjacent to Faraday.

A classic Aboriginal water well. Dja Dja Wurrung district.

Aboriginals grinding stone. Loddon district. Picture by Bill Davies.

1. Images to the right are:
2. Example of a scar tree, Loddon District.
3. A Rock well and grinding stone, Vaughn area.
4. A possible corroborree site. This natural stone formation may have had meaning to the Aboriginal people. A long stone impression of Myndi is nearby. Bealiba district.
5. An example of a sacred birthing tree, an important cultural site for Aboriginal People. This tree was the birthplace of countless Aboriginal children over the several hundred years of it's existence. It is in the Coliban District and, to protect it, it's location will not be revealed.
6. A ring tree on the banks of the Loddon River. These were grafted by the Indigenous peoples and are believed to be signposts or signals.

An extremely rare coloured lantern slide of a canoe tree at Harcourt, a remnant of which is still standing beside the main street. The date and photographer are unknown, but the horse and jinker suggest early days.

Part Two

The Land and its Squatters

When Britain first took possession of Australia, their government had no idea of the potential for wealth that the land offered. They had no inkling of the extent of the land or whether it was an island or a continent. But they knew it would be a useful location to establish a remote convict colony. There was a growing need to clear the overcrowded prisons, since America was no longer available following its declaration of independence in 1776.

And so it was to be – a tiny settlement on the east coast was eminently suitable. The British statesmen had little or no interest in Australia, other than as a dumping ground for their unwanted people. They appointed a Governor, then later on Governors, to run the show, giving them unilateral powers. The Governor was the law and was generous in handing out great parcels of land to friends as rewards for services. This continued until 1831, when the Home Government finally woke up. By then, almost four million acres of New South Wales had been given away. Australia wide, a total of about seven million acres had been handed out, either at no cost or for a trifling amount.

Consider this: The Australian Agricultural Company, set up in England by Royal Charter, was given 1,000,000 acres for no cost. Their website states that:

> 'In 1824, AACo was established as a land development company with the assistance of the British Parliament's Crown Grant of 1,000,000 acres in the Port Stephens area of the Colony of New South Wales.'

The company is still operating today. Similarly, the Van Diemen's Land Company gained 250,000 acres for a mere four hundred and sixty eight pounds quit-rent, a form of tax.

From Wikipedia:

> The Van Diemen's Land Company (also known as Van Dieman Land Company) is a farming corporation in the Australian state of Tasmania. It was founded in 1825 and received a royal charter the same year, and was granted 250,000 acres. (1,000 square kilometres) in northwest Van Diemen's Land (now Tasmania) in 1826. The company was a group of London merchants who planned a wool growing venture to supply the needs of the British textile industry.

By the time settlers arrived in the Port Phillip District, the rules had changed and a rental of about ten pounds a year was payable. But the squatter could select as much land as he wanted for that.

The word 'squatter' originated in America to describe a person who occupied land without legal right. That also applied in Australia in the early days, but by the 1820s it had quite a different meaning. In Australia, a squatter was, and remains, a person who owns or leases large tracts of land to raise sheep and cattle.

From 1831, if public land was sold, the price was fixed at five shillings per acre. In 1838 it was raised to twelve shillings per acre and then later to one pound per acre. Then some clever British statesman ruled that anybody handing over five thousand pounds could take 5,000 acres anywhere, but not within five miles of a town. Wealthy men rapidly seized upon this. Henry Dendy brought what is now the Melbourne suburb of Brighton and surrounds – eight square miles. Within twenty-four hours he was offered fifteen thousand pounds for it, which he declined. Joseph Elgar selected what are now the suburbs of Hawthorn, Kew and Camberwell. Governor Gipps was quick to realise what was happening and put a prompt stop to it.

Early White Settlers Arrive on Dja Dja Wurrung Land

In early 1824, Hamilton Hume and William Hovell set out from Sydney on an expedition to locate new grazing lands. They headed south-west from near Lake George and journeyed to far-off Port Phillip. They travelled for many months, passing through vast areas of the most impressively fertile land. When they returned to Sydney, the two argued in public over what they had done and seen and, as a result, their journey was largely ignored for years. Some small expeditions were made in the following years, but it wasn't until Major Thomas Mitchell's third expedition in 1836 that any serious endeavour occurred.

Mitchell's expedition into the interior took his group to the land which he later named *Australia Felix*. It was explored and surveyed in careful detail. Mitchell went on to write the following words about his 'discovery' of the land now known as central and western Victoria:

> 'We had at length discovered a country ready for the immediate reception of civilised man; and destined perhaps to become eventually a portion of a great empire. ... Flocks might be turned out upon its hills, or the plough at once set to work in the plains. ... As I stood, the first European intruder on the sublime solitude of these verdant plains as yet untouched by flocks or herds, I felt conscious of being the harbinger of mighty changes; and that our steps would soon be followed by the men and the animals for which it seemed to have been prepared. ... I named this region Australia Felix, the better to distinguish it from the parched deserts of the interior country where we had wandered so unprofitably and so long. ... Certainly a land more favourable for colonisation could not be found.

This revelation would change the land we love forever.

Much has been written about Mitchell's third expedition. Our focus is on his arrival in central Victoria. This area of land extends from the Pyrenees to a little south of the mountain we now call Mount Alexander, which Mitchell initially named Mount Byng, after an officer he served with in the Peninsular war. He later renamed it after Alexander the Great, King

*Hills of lava, or Mammeloid Hills, from Mount Greenock.
On the horizon is Mount Byng Pass (Mount Alexander).
From Mitchell's Journal.*

of Macedonia, in his mind to better tie this area together. He had named the large mountain to the south Mount Macedon, realising this coastal range mountain was near to the newly colonised Port Phillip District, previously named after Governor Arthur Phillip. With Alexander the Great's father also named Phillip, Mitchell saw a connection and decided to tie the three places together. Mitchell named the river that forms the extreme eastern boundary of the Dja Dja Wurrung country, Campaspe after Alexander the Great's lover and prominent citizen of Larissa in Thessaly.[1]

It was 24th September 1836 when Major Mitchell's party entered what is the traditional western boundary of the Dja Dja Wurrung people's land. Mitchell's party had camped just outside what was later named Burnbank (and is now Lexton) at the base of what he identified as Theodolite Hill.

Mitchell wrote in his journal:

> 'Having passed over the swampy bed of the rivulet flowing southwards, we at length encamped near a round hill [Theodolite Hill], which being clear on the summit, was therefore a favourable station for the theodolite. This hill also consisted of granite, and commanded an open and extensive view over the country to the east.'

While on top of Theodolite Hill, Mitchell carefully charted and plotted a course though the valleys and hills that lay to the east. On arriving at what is today called Lexton on 25th September 1836, he wrote:

---

1 Mitchell's Journal. (In 1985 Margaret Oulton wrote an excellent history of the Shire of Lexton which she titled *A Valley of The Finest Description*.)

'One bold range of forest land appeared before us, and after crossing it, we passed over several rivulets falling north, then over a ridge of trapean conglomerate with embedded quartz pebbles, and descended into a valley of the finest description[2]. Grassy hills clear of timber appeared beyond a stream also flowing to the Northward, These hills consisted of old vesicular lava.'

Mitchell had entered an area that would be settled a year later by an overland party representing Henry Boucher Bowerman. He was a well-to-do retired military man from Parramatta, and a good friend of Major Mitchell. He named the area Maiden Hills.

Our family is proud to record that our forebear, Abraham Braybrook, a convict servant, was one of that party, making him one of the very first white settlers in the district beyond Castlemaine. We shall hear more of these people later, but now we follow Mitchell's journey on his way toward what was to become Castlemaine.

On 26th September, Mitchell's party arrived at what he named Mount Greenock, an extinct volcano, south of what is now Talbot. He rode to its summit and made a sketch of the scene that lay to the east, naming the surrounding hills the Mammeloid Hills.[3]

'... I enjoyed such a charming view eastward from the summit as can but seldom fall to the lot of the explorers of new countries. The surface presented the forms of pristine beauty clothed in the hues of spring; and the shining verdure of these smooth and symmetrical hills was relieved by the darker hues of the wood with which they were interlaced; which exhibited every variety of tint, from a dark brown in the foreground to a light blue in extreme distance.'

'...The hills consisted entirely of lava and I named them from their peculiar shape the Mammeloid hills, and the station on which I stood Mount Greenock.'

---

2   Stapyleton's Journal.
3   Mitchell named them the Mammeloid Hills because he considered their shape to be that of a reclining woman's breasts.

Mitchell and his second in command, Granville Stapylton, were later to say that this was the most beautiful and best sheep country they had ever seen. Stapylton considered Batman's purchase of 600,000 acres ridiculous, but in dreaming about the magnificent Burnbank Valley at Lexton, a grant for himself did not seem at all unfitting.

On the night of the 27th September 1836, Mitchell's party camped at Splitters Creek which runs at the base of Mount Cameron, north of present day Clunes. Visitors to this site today will see that it is almost as it was in 1836. The description Mitchell gives matches perfectly. He also wrote:

> 'I was surprised to hear the voice of a Scotchwoman in the camp this morning. The peculiar accent and rapid utterance could not be mistaken as I thought, and I called to inquire who the stranger was, when I ascertained that it was only Tommy Came-last who was imitating a Scotch female who, as I then learnt, was at Portland Bay and had been very kind to Tommy. The imitation was ridiculously true through all the modulations of that peculiar accent although, strange to say, without the pronunciation of a single intelligible word.'

Mitchell's writing continued:

> 'While the party went forward over the open plains with Mr. Stapylton I ascended a smooth round hill (Mount Cameron), distant about a mile to the southward of our camp, from which I could with ease continue my survey by means of hills on all sides, the highest of them being to the southward. I could trace the rivulets flowing northward into one or two principal channels, near several masses of mountain: these channels and ranges being probably connected with those crossed by us on our route from the Murray.'

Mitchell always appeared to know exactly where he was and apparently was never lost. He continued over the Moolort plains, crossed the Loddon River and came to camp in what is now the site of Newstead, either behind the current post office or below the site of the cairn erected to honour him on the edge of town, depending on which local you listen to.

Mitchell left the following morning and headed towards the present site of Castlemaine.

It is interesting to note that Mount Alexander, as visited by Mitchell in 1836, was only sparsely covered with timber, unlike today. This is also clearly shown in pre-gold rush drawings. There is also the fact that Mitchell was able to clearly observe Mount Macedon from the mountain's summit.

***

Many settlers arrived in the Coliban area in the first few years of white settlement, including Charles Ebden, William Yaldwyn, William Mollison, and William Bowman. Our descriptions are far from complete, but more detailed accounts are available in several publications.

Charles Hotson Ebden

Charles Ebden, born in the Cape Colony in 1811, was the first of the 'white invasion' settlers on the Campaspe River, arriving in May 1837. He established Karlsruhe Station (his original spelling) close to the Campaspe River, on land that he said reminded him more of England than did the Murray area. He drew the property name from his old college in Germany. We will use the current spelling.

Ebden actually made his way to Carlsruhe in stages, first establishing a temporary run on the Murray River that he named Mungabareena (now Albury) and a second named Bonegilla, also on the Murray. His selection at Carlsruhe totalled about 35,000 acres.

Charles Hotson Ebden (1811-1867)

He was a true entrepreneur, a smart investor and a relentless businessman. Records show that by July 1838, he had 8,000 sheep and 1,800 cattle on the station. He also had ten free men (paid workers) plus twenty-two assigned convicts providing free labour. He bought a great deal of land at the first Melbourne land sales which ultimately produced hugely profitable returns.

Around this time he entered into a partnership with James Donnithorne to raise more money. It was very successful and in 1839 Donnithorne took over the entire Carlsruhe property which then held approximately 9,000 sheep. This deal gave Ebden a recorded profit of twenty-four thousand pounds and additional saleable assets of thirty-four thousand pounds – the latter assets actually totalled a massive forty thousand pounds; quite a tidy return in just two years.

He retired to a large home in Collingwood, and in 1851 he purchased Campaspe Plains Station of 144,000 acres. He sold this in 1855 and took his wife and family to England for a visit.

When he returned he bought a group of stations around the Loddon River and west of the Murray. In all, he either owned, or part owned, ten properties, including Murrabit, Lake Boga, Quambatook and Pental Island. In total, this amounted to about 400,000 acres stocked with 1,500 cattle and 52,000 sheep.

In October 1867 he collapsed and died at his beloved Melbourne Club, leaving behind one hundred thousand pounds, plus a number of excellent properties. He was, as he once said, 'disgustingly rich'.

* * *

The following amazing, little known story is condensed from JO Randell's, *Pastoral Settlements in Northern Victoria*, Volume 1. It is connected to Ebden's overland party, as the characters in the story were in Ebden's employ.

While Ebden and his team were at a temporary station near the Goulburn River, two bushrangers induced George Comerford, John Dignum and several other convict workers to join them. The group absconded and resolved to walk to South Australia.

By the time they arrived at a small creek below Mount Alexander, west of the Coliban River, they had run out of food. Dignum and Comerford decided to stretch the meagre supply of provisions by murdering their companions.

As the six men slept, they were quickly killed in cold blood with an axe and guns. Lighting a large fire, Comerford and Dignum threw the corpses into the flames where they were largely, but not completely, consumed.

Travelling south, they got a job at Aitken's station near Gisborne, but after a short time they were discovered and arrested, not for murder, but for absconding.

Somehow the pair escaped. Before long they had a serious and violent disagreement and parted company. Soon after, Comerford was arrested in Albury.

Eventually, Dignum was also caught. Both men were taken to Sydney where Comerford confessed to the Mount Alexander murders. He was taken back to Port Phillip and from there to the murder site where a search of the ashes revealed human teeth, hair and bones. Some of the skulls were untouched. On the return ride to Port Phillip, Comerford seized a constable's gun, fatally shot him, stole his horse and escaped.

In January 1838, he obtained work at Howey's Station on Jackson's Creek. In an argument, he threatened three convict workers with death. They overpowered him and the law was summoned. He was taken to Sydney for trial on two counts of murder, and found guilty. Comerford was hung for his part in the grisly murders he had confessed to.

His accomplice, Dignum, was in jail awaiting trial, this time for horse stealing. He had some luck on his side. Because Comerford was dead, there were no witnesses to the Mount Alexander murders, so no murder trial was considered. However, for horse theft, he was sent to Norfolk Island for life – possibly a fate worse than death.

This murderous affair took place near what is Stratford Lodge homestead on Coliban Park Road.

In August 1853, it was reported[4] that John Hepburn found what he believed to be the skull of one of the murder victims at the junction of Forest and Barkers Creek, Castlemaine. If so, it was probably taken there by Aboriginal people. We do not know if this is correct, but Hepburn was a man of excellent reputation and honour and it was his firm belief.

William Yaldwyn

Closely following Charles Ebden were Alexander Mollison and William Yaldwyn, both in December 1837. Actually, Yaldwyn arrived around

---

4   McBride, TF, 1898. *Letters from Victorian Pioneers ... to Charles Joseph La Trobe.*

four months after his overseer, John Coppock, had led the main party and selected the land on Yaldwyn's behalf, but the honour of being the second squatter went to the master.

William Yaldwyn was born into privilege and riches in Sussex England in 1801. He inherited the family estate and its financial burdens when he came of age. He enjoyed a lavish lifestyle.

William Yaldwyn arrived in Sydney in October 1836. With him were his pregnant wife Henrietta and two sons. Early in 1837 he prepared for the long overland drive to Port Phillip and was ready for the departure in April of that year. As he wished to remain with his wife until her confinement, he engaged John Coppock to head the drive and to actually select land for him. He would follow later in a covered wagon accompanied by two servants whose exclusive role was to serve his needs. They were not involved in driving stock.

At the time, Edward Eyre, well known for his later explorations, was also preparing a drive to Port Phillip with a good number of sheep and cattle. His objective was to sell the stock at Port Phillip settlement, where there was strong demand.

Coppock and Eyre set out in tandem from Yass, parting company at the Goulburn River when Eyre proceeded to Port Phillip and sold his stock at a handsome profit.

William Henry Yaldwyn (1801–1866)

Coppock was responsible for several thousand sheep and about 300 cattle. After several adventures and misadventures, the Coppock party arrived in the Coliban district in July 1837.

Coppock then went about selecting land for Yaldwyn. He chose very well. The selection amounted to approximately 51,000 acres (some 80 square miles). It was possibly the choicest land to be found anywhere in *Australia Felix*. Importantly, it was well watered – the western boundary being the Coliban River, with the Campaspe River and Pipers Creek running through it. The only neighbour was Charles Ebden to the south.

Coppock chose to erect the head station on the west side of the Campaspe River. There has been a good deal of confusion and conflicting

An original outbuilding on Barfold station, east of the river, built about 1860. Its use is not known. *Remnants of the second Barfold homestead to the west of the River. It replaced the original slab hut.*

opinion on this over the ensuing years. In 1840, George Robinson, Chief Protector of Aborigines, placed it on the east side, but on the same day Assistant Protector Edward Parker placed it on the west side in a drawing he made! Our research confirms that it was on the west side.

The original hut was replaced by a more substantial stone structure soon after. The remains of this building still stand, mostly intact, and definitely on the west side of the river. The first building is said to have been made from pre-cut slabs and had four rooms. It possibly had a bark roof, as was common at the time.

It appears likely that the more elaborate second home was later abandoned by a future owner (WHF Mitchell), and an impressive stone building erected on the east side of the Campaspe. Regrettably, this was destroyed by fire around 1920. The present homestead[5] features a stone wall retained from the fire-razed predecessor.

Meanwhile, Yaldwyn made his way south from Yass after his wife had borne him a daughter. His party included an additional five assigned convicts to look after 1800 sheep. He was comfortably accommodated in his two-horse, covered wagon and was well attended by his servants. It was not an eventful journey, except when they came upon two human skeletons. Yaldwyn was convinced that they were white men who had

---

5 The present Barfold Estate, now a boutique winery, is not to be compared to Barfold Homestead which is located along Mitchell Lane, south of the Barfold township.

been killed and eaten by the Aboriginals. Conveying his belief to his men did nothing to quieten their fear of the Indigenous People.

On his arrival, he was delighted with Coppock's selection and promptly named the property Barfold. The name is derived from their English residence on farmland near an riverbank.[6]

It was soon to be a flourishing enterprise. The report of the Crown Lands Department of 1838 showed that Barfold held 4,000 sheep and 300 cattle. In addition there were 18 assigned convict workers.

Yaldwyn did not spend a great deal of time at the property, preferring instead to reside in the comfort of a home in Melbourne. His wife and three children had soon made their way to join him, travelling by ship.

Among Yaldwyn's many social and community activities in town, he was one of the 23 founders of the very exclusive Melbourne Mechanics Institution (now called the Melbourne Athenaeum), which to this day remains as exclusive as ever.

It was while he was absent in Melbourne that an ugly event involving Aborigines occurred. It is a happening that lives on in infamy and is probably an extreme example of the atrocities committed on the Aboriginal people by white invaders.

It is worth considering that these were brutal times, when life was cheap, particularly for the lower classes. Much of the Aboriginal People's traditional foods had been removed by indiscriminate slaughter of kangaroos, birds and fish, and by sheep, which destroyed the root of murnong, a staple food. The resultant food shortage led to some Aboriginal people stealing 'jumbucks' for food. Retaliation was often disastrous. It was such an event on 9th June 1838 that led to the attack at Waterloo Flat, headed by John Coppock, the overseer of Barfold.

At the outstation, about seven miles from the head station, two shepherds were pursued by a fairly large group of Aboriginal men. They fled, fearing for their lives, and a number of sheep were driven off to be killed and eaten. On hearing about this, Coppock was furious and gathered together a group of men, mounted them on horses and rode off to locate the sheep and the offenders. They came upon the party of Aboriginal people at Waterloo Flat where they had already killed a number of sheep

---

6   According to the British Ordnance Survey, there is also a place called Barfold not far from the Yaldwyn's stately manor Blackdown.

Below this tree-topped hill lies the site of the Waterloo Flat Massacre.

and were roasting them on large fires. They had also broken the legs of other sheep to prevent them from running off.

Nobody will ever know the entire truth, but, according to Coppock, the Aboriginal men began throwing spears at them, and they retaliated in self defence. Shots were fired, estimated by one convict witness as 'ninety lead rounds' and he saw 'eight or nine' Aboriginal men lying dead.

Coppock ordered the men to throw the bodies onto the fires and then herd the sheep back to the outstation. Coppock stated that he feared an ambush all the way, as it was becoming dark, but nothing happened.

The next morning, they returned to the site. The camp was deserted and the bodies had been partly burnt. The fires were stoked and the remains completely destroyed. Although there was an investigation, no action was taken against the white men.

A similar incident occurred in July 1839. There was theft of a quantity of sheep from Darlington Station. Cox, the station manager, led a search party and found the sheep and the thieves at an unidentified location. There was 'a measure of force', but no further information is available.

However, there is a long-surviving local story at Mia Mia that may or may not be related to this event. The area was home to a group of Indigenous people, and there was a large number of traditional mia mia shelters there, which gave the place its name. According to the story, a number of Aboriginal people had been shot by a party of men and their bodies thrown into a waterhole behind what is now the Mia Mia public school. There is no proof, but if it is true, it is likely that Cox and his party were the offenders.

John Pascoe Fawkner wrote a scathing article in his newspaper condemning the actions of the party involved. It is curious that no inquiry took place, even though it is certain that Aboriginal men were killed.[7]

Yaldwyn did not stay long at Barfold, preferring life in Melbourne Town, looking out for the many investment opportunities that arose. He purchased a considerable amount of land in the first land sales held in Melbourne and acquired leasehold properties in other districts. He and his family resided in a quality brick home in Russell Street.

Toward the end of 1839, Yaldwyn sold Barfold to Thomas Thornloe, a Tasmanian acting for Sir George Arthur and his associate John Montagu. He had de-stocked the property and is said to have sold it for two hundred pounds. Not a large sum, even in 1839, but in reality all he had to sell was a humble house, a few sheds and workers' humpies and the lease on the land.

Soon after the sale of Barfold he took the family home to England, and on his return he moved to Queensland where he served six years as a Member of the Legislative Council. He died in 1866 while visiting Sydney.

Sir George Arthur and John Montagu

Of Sir George Arthur and John Montagu, who purchased Barfold in partnership, it is difficult to decide who was the more inhumane, or untrustworthy. Sir George Arthur was appointed Lieutenant-Governor of Van Diemen's Land (Tasmania) in 1824 and then began the harshest administration of any colony. The most appropriate word to describe him is 'despot'; he fits every interpretation of it. He established the notorious Port Arthur Convict Prison where some of the inmates were often pleased to die so as to escape the brutality and dreadful conditions.

---

7   Within a day of this, neighbour Henry Monro was speared by Aboriginal men when he rode his horse full pelt into a group of them. He was very seriously injured but survived.

Before his arrival as Governor, no person had been hanged in Tasmania, but during the period of his reign, 1824–1836, Arthur oversaw the execution of 260 prisoners. He also started the Black War which was intended to drive all Indigenous people to isolated peninsulas where they could be 'controlled'. He declared Martial Law and issued a proclamation that 'any person may arm and join with the military to drive them (the Aboriginal people) to a safe distance, treating them as open enemies.' He often used the word 'warfare' in his official communications. And if it were a war, perhaps it is appropriate to use the term 'lest we forget'.

Sir George Arthur (1784–1854).

It can be said with some justification that Arthur contributed significantly to the almost total extinction of the Tasmanian Aboriginal people.

In connection with this operation, he oversaw a blatantly corrupt law enforcement system, where money and privilege changed hands on a regular basis.

Andrew Bent was the publisher and editor of the *Hobart Town Gazette*. When Arthur ordered him not to print anything detrimental or critical of his government, Bent refused to comply. Arthur had the legal power to order a halt to any printing, under the Newspaper Licensing Act. Bent's refusal to comply led to him being hounded and persecuted by Sir George, and he was even jailed for alleged libel of the Governor. Finally, Bent succumbed to the onslaught and quit, a broken man. However, in 1829, the Home Government repealed the Newspaper Licensing

---

Colonial Times Office, March 23, 1826.
☞ *In the proceedings of Mr. Attorney-General Gellibrand's case, published on Wednesday last, it is in numerous instances unequivocally asserted by Mr. Evan Henry Thomas, as a witness before the Commissioners of Inquiry, that he "resigned" his employment upon my Newspaper. In reply to Mr. Thomas's false assertions in this respect, I take the earliest opportunity of stating, that, so far from Mr. Thomas resigning, I was unavoidably compelled to dispense with his services, in consequence of the libellous tendency of his writings, which have been, and are, productive of so much inconvenience to me. And, while I am thus prosecuted for publishing his writings, he himself having been called as a witness against me on my trial for the same, has recently received a large grant of land from the Government! The facts of his dismissal by me, which was particularly caused by my refusing to insert a most violent article, can be proved by two or three persons, who were present at the time I settled with Mr. Thomas, " in full of all demands," and when his services were as repeatedly refused, as they were attempted to be forced upon me.* A. BENT.

Act, and for a brief period Bent resumed his writing with the *Colonial Times*. He wrote: 'Freedom of the press is now restored to the colony of Tasmania.' But he was unable to continue.

Meanwhile, Arthur grew very rich as he speculated in land and business. Among his activities, he established the Bank of Hobart which, by 1841, held two-thirds of the mortgages in Tasmania. Many of these were cashed in by the bank when a depression hit around that time. Although he was by now living in England, Arthur remained the major shareholder.

There was a collective sigh of relief when Sir George Arthur was recalled to England, an extremely wealthy man. He was the ultimate wheeler and dealer, and anybody who denied or defied him was made to suffer. He departed Hobart early in 1837, farewelled from the wharf by a huge crowd, thankful to see him gone.

Arthur's associate was John Montagu, a man of equally questionable character who arrived in Tasmania at the same time as George Arthur. Montagu had a position as a clerk in the government but quickly made his way up through the ranks. We are not sure how this came about, but a cynic might connect his rise to the fact that he married a niece of Sir George Arthur.

Montagu was given a series of cosy jobs, eventually being made the Colonial Secretary – in other words Secretary to the Lieutenant-Governor, the second most powerful position in the colony. He was closely involved in the workings of the Newspaper Licensing Act, used so effectively and ruthlessly against Andrew Bent.

In 1828 he received a grant of 2,560 acres of prime land, courtesy of the Governor, and in 1832 he was appointed Acting Treasurer. Sir George and he worked closely together to find various ways of gathering wealth, something they did with much success.

Another clerk, Thomas Thurloe, became friendly with Arthur and Montagu and became a trusted servant. In 1836-37, they despatched Thurloe to Port Phillip to investigate investment opportunities. To begin with, Thurloe established a leasehold station near present day

John Montagu
1797–1853

Craigieburn and stocked it with sheep and cattle brought across Bass Strait. Soon afterwards, he purchased Barfold for Arthur and Montagu from Yaldwyn whom he came to know in Melbourne, possibly through the Melbourne Mechanics Institution.

When Sir George Arthur was recalled to England in 1836–37, he appointed Montagu to manage his many financial affairs, including Barfold station.[8]

It is difficult to decide which of the two, George Arthur or John Montagu, I regard as the more undesirable, but Arthur must be first choice.

It is unlikely that either of them ever set foot on Barfold, their only interest in the place was almost certainly profit.

With Sir George back in England, Montagu was, no doubt, on the lookout for a well-heeled buyer for Barfold Station as part of finalising the affairs of Sir George Arthur and himself. Onto the scene came a friend and fellow government employee.

William Henry Fancourt Mitchell

Mitchell was English, born into a 'good' family in 1797, but began life in the colony in 1833 as a humble government clerk. He rose rapidly through the ranks, almost certainly assisted by a family connection with Governor Arthur. Under Governor Franklin, his rise continued and by 1839 he was the Assistant Colonial Secretary at a significant four hundred pounds per annum. John Montagu was his superior.

In 1842, Mitchell resigned and crossed to Port Phillip where he purchased the leasehold of Barfold station. The purchase price is unknown, but, being well stocked, it was likely to have been considerable, generating an excellent profit for Arthur and Montagu.

Mitchell stocked the station with stud sheep of the best quality, but soon decided that they were unsuited to the Barfold climate and sold them, at profit, to the wealthy, Scottish-born Learmonth brothers of Ercildoune Station. Cost meant little to the brothers, as long as they had the best.

---

8   The newly appointed Governor Franklin and Montagu did not see eye to eye. They were involved in a bitter and prolonged dispute which ultimately caused them both to be recalled to England.

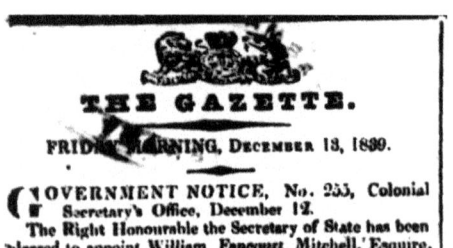

THE GAZETTE.

FRIDAY MORNING, DECEMBER 13, 1839.

GOVERNMENT NOTICE, No. 255, Colonial Secretary's Office, December 12.
The Right Honourable the Secretary of State has been pleased to appoint William Fancourt Mitchell, Esquire, to the office of Assistant Colonial Secretary to this Government.

By His Excellency's command,
M. FORSTER.

The New Secretary.
Amongst the English Intelligence, inserted last week, was a paragraph, mentioning an interview, which "Mr. J. Montagu" had with Lord Normanby; we were struck, at the time, with the circumstance, and augured something "new and strange," as the consequence. Lo! It hath happened! Mr. William Fancourt Mitchell has been appointed to the "new and strange" office of *Assistant Colonial Secretary* :—" *risum teneatis amici?*" or, in plain English, who can help laughing?

In 1845, Mitchell extended his holdings with a lease of 65,000 acres forming Terrick Terrick station between Bendigo and the Murray.

In 1852, he purchased 640 acres of the Barfold leasehold run for the homestead area. Later that year he sold part of his leasehold west of the Campaspe (Stratford Lodge) to James Orr. In 1853, Governor Latrobe appointed him as the chief of the police force, so he hired a manager for Barfold station and moved to Melbourne where his strong interest in the land continued. In 1856 he purchased 4,500 acres of the Barfold leasehold, adding to the 640 acre homestead block.

William Mitchell (by then Sir William) continued to occupy important government positions. In 1856 he was made a Member of the Legislative Council and Post Master General and then the Commissioner for Railways. He died at Barfold in November 1884 ending a fascinating chapter in the history of that property. The last piece of Barfold was sold to JS Osborne in 1897.

Alexander Fullerton Mollison

The son of an established Scottish merchant, Alexander Fullerton Mollison was born in London in 1805. He had a good education, presumably in connection with surveying. On his arrival in Sydney in May 1834, he began work with a party of surveyors in the Bathurst district. It was here he saw the wealth of prosperous farmers and graziers and realised the potential available.

He was known as a man of integrity, good humour and, with an adventurous streak, he quickly contemplated exploring beyond the settled area bounded by the remote township of Yass.

Sometime early in 1836, he took a ship to Hobart and then to Port Phillip, probably to investigate the opportunities.

On his return to Sydney, he formed a partnership with several friends whose entire purpose was to assemble stock to take south to Port Phillip District to acquire rich land so readily available. The partners purchased Uriara station specifically to assemble and hold stock in readiness for an overland journey. Uriara was within the settled area and Mollison was therefore entitled to engage a good number of convict servants – free labour. It was a common practice to take convicts from within the approved area southwards, without permission, with no questions asked.

Alexander Fullerton Mollison 1805–1885

The group was ready and set out for Port Phillip in early April 1837 with about 600 cattle, five thousand sheep and 49 convict workers.

Thus began what was to be a very long and difficult journey. To begin with, the crossing of the Murrumbidgee River was difficult. The river was too swift to swim the sheep across, so they built a bridge by putting the drays end to end with their shafts and poles propped up with wooden stakes. The floors were then covered with green bushes and tarpaulins covered with dirt. This formed a reasonable pathway which the sheep crossed with ease. It was a lengthy task but was very successful.

After encountering more difficulties, the group arrived at the Murray River. Here they met their most serious impediment to date. Again, there had been heavy rain upstream, and the river flowed strongly. Swimming the sheep across was not an option.

The cattle were forced to swim and, luckily, there were only a few losses. For the sheep, Mollison ordered the men to convert the drays into punts. They attached numerous empty casks to the heavy vehicles for buoyancy and the sheep were transported forty at a time. It was an exercise that took ten full days to complete.

Because of the many problems and delays, plus the fact that they were running short of supplies, Mollison decided to leave almost the entire party at Indigo Creek. On 12th July, he, with 2 drays and five of the men, moved forward to Port Phillip for supplies. This didn't prove to be as easy as they expected. They ran into more problems with flooding streams. The Ovens River was in flood, which meant unloading all the goods on the drays and floating them across on a homemade tarpaulin punt. On 17th July, the Broken River was running high and was crossed with great difficulty. The Goulburn River was also in flood and the current swift. They managed to rig a flying fox to move goods across. The drays were disassembled and sent across by canoe.

On 25th July, they came across John Coppock at Barfold and then moved on to Ebden's Carlsruhe Station where they borrowed stores. These were loaded onto bullocks in packs, and two of the men headed back to Indigo Creek with the food and goods, by now urgently needed.

Proceeding to Port Phillip, Mollison purchased supplies and, on 5th August, began the journey back to Indigo Creek, arriving without serious incident. By September, the group had moved to Bontharambo where Mollison called a halt for the lambing. On 5th October, he finally resumed the journey with part of his stock and men – about 1,100 sheep and a large mob of cattle. By 25th October they crossed the now subdued Broken River and by 16th November arrived at McIvor Creek (Heathcote).

Soon after, they reached the Campaspe River below present day Redesdale. They crossed it at what Mollison described as 'a rivulet in a deep glen', which is an apt description.

From there, with three of his workers, he rode on a tour of inspection of the region, looking for a suitable run. In all they were away for a week, covering about 150 miles. The quartet first rode west before turning south to as far as the Werribee River. They returned via Aitken's run at Gisborne. From there they proceeded to where the others had camped with the animals and equipment at Redesdale. Finally he re-joined the party he had left waiting near Redesdale and selected land totalling about 60,000 acres adjoining the Ebden property. It took in the present town of Trentham and half of Malmsbury and Taradale townships. He built the head station a few hundred metres from the west bank of the Campaspe River at what is now Malmsbury.

Alexander Mollison was known to have been kind to the Aboriginal people and, unlike many others, in all his time in the district had no violent or threatening encounters with them. He described them as 'inoffensive and trustworthy'.

It was 5th December 1837. Because of the many delays on their journey, Mollison and his party were the third settlers to arrive in the Coliban district. They could well have been the second.

William Hutchinson (Bowman's interesting partner)

William Hutchinson, born in England in 1772, was quite a remarkable character. In 1796 he was convicted of stealing and sentenced to death, which was commuted to seven years in NSW. He arrived aboard the *Hillsborough* in 1799. He was then convicted of stealing from government stores and sent to the dreaded Norfolk Island.

How he emerged from there and came to be engaged in the public service is not known, but he quickly rose through the ranks, and by 1803 he was Superintendent of Convicts on the island. Somehow he accumulated a good amount of property and there established a successful trade in pork with the government. In 1813–14, he is reputed to have played an important role in the abandonment of Norfolk Island.

Back in Sydney he was appointed Superintendent of Convicts and Public Works and he became a good friend of Governor Macquarie and a man of influence. His post put him in charge of taking valuables and money from all newly arrived convicts. He then invested it in businesses. He was obviously an unscrupulous man and was soon accused of abuse of his powers and was replaced in 1823. At the time he was also under suspicion of misuse of money and possessions of newly arrived convicts.

Following this he was somehow appointed as principal wharfinger, the equivalent of today's harbour master. This placed him in complete control of all goods received and despatched from the wharf, with all the opportunities that presented.

Hutchinson continued to forge the good life, undeterred by any criticism and became a financier and a founder of the Bank of New South Wales. He had a finger in many property pies and was a partner in a large flour mill. Hutchinson had property interests throughout Sydney and in Moss Vale, Sutton Forest, Bargo and Bong Bong. When he died in 1846 he left twenty thousand pounds. As was customary, his real estate and other assets were not listed, but undoubtedly they were worth a pretty penny.

... and his mate William Bowman

Here is another interesting character. It has been alleged that Bowman boasted to have shot every Aboriginal person on his run! True or false we will never know, but it is unlikely.

He was the son of William Bowman who farmed a substantial land grant at Windsor west of Sydney. Through his father, young William had friends in high places. In 1828 he had a pub at Bong Bong. With the growth of Berrima, the township of Bong Bong was bypassed by a new road, and the town died, and the hotel business collapsed. He was awarded a 640 acre piece of land as compensation from a friendly government. This set him up, and it was all upwards from then on. He married the daughter of William Hutchinson (see above) and he soon became quite wealthy. His father-in-law had considerable property in the Murrumbidgee district.

By 1837, Bowman, no doubt assisted by Hutchinson, had established a station at Tarrawingee (east of Wangaratta, Victoria), stocked with 5,000 sheep.

Early in 1838 he headed an overland party looking for land to settle in the Port Phillip District. He joined up with another two parties on a similar mission – Captain John Hepburn and brothers John and William Coghill. That group had 2,000 sheep. They proceeded southwards with few problems. They had feared the Aboriginal people, but had no encounters with them. Three of Bowman's assigned men were brave enough to complain that, as the group leaders, they worked harder than the rest. It is said that Bowman was not impressed with their insolence and personally flogged the trio brutally. 'They behaved well the rest of the trip,' he said later.

In mid-March, Bowman selected about 80,000 acres of rich property with frontages on the west bank of the Coliban River, alongside Ebden, Mollison and Yaldwyn. This was later to become Sutton Grange and Stratford Lodge. His partner, William Hutchinson, was not active but preferred to remain in the finance and land dealing business.

Henry Monro

Another of the first settlers in the Coliban District was Scottish-born Henry Monro who arrived in Australia in 1833. He was obviously a man of considerable wealth, with good contacts in high places. We assume this because he came from a highly regarded medical family, both his father and grandfather were held in high esteem.

By 1833, Monro had acquired land at Boro Creek just south of Goulburn where he held a small, leased property. However he must have had a larger lease nearby, as he was entitled to hold a good number of convict workers.

By early 1838, he was ready to make the journey down the Major's Line[9] to the Port Phillip district to seek his fortune in sheep and cattle. He brought with him an unknown number of sheep and cattle, as well as about twenty convict workers.

Monro did very well. By mid-1838 he settled for a lease of about 45,000 acres of land that eventually would become Campaspe Station and Spring Plains Station. The property was bounded by Captain Sylvester Brown's Darlington Station and Yaldwyn's Barfold Station. It appears that he did not name his run, and it was generally referred to as Monro's Plains or Monro's Run.

A short distance downstream from the old iron bridge at Redesdale is the stony ford over the Campaspe River. It was always known as Monro's Crossing, but lately is referred to as the Old Ford. It is certainly on Monro's land and possibly was his crossing place. The stones that make up the ford appear to have been carried there, most likely by the assigned convicts who worked so hard for no pay on Monro's Plains.

For the first year or more, these early arrivals had virtually the entire area for themselves. It was a tough life and it was also a time of common brutality. The place he chose for his head station had already witnessed a bloody massacre of about eight Aboriginal people by men from Yaldwyn and Bowman's stations – Waterloo Flat.

Monro established the head station just west of the Coliban River, we believe it was close to the old homestead of the present day Coliban Estate.

---

9   The Major's Line refers to the wheel-tracks left by Mitchells' exploring party on its return journey from Victoria's Western District in 1836.

In about 1839 he built a comfortable new homestead from upright slabs, with six rooms and a detached kitchen. It later became Spring Plains Station. In 1840, the original home was described as a deserted hut.

By that year he had some 4,000 sheep and 300 cattle, and the station was prosperous. It was well established, with fenced paddocks for the cultivation of wheat close to the homestead. The soil was rich, with little timber to clear. It grew vegetables, and fruit trees thrived, and it even had its own small, hand-operated flour mill. The station had a population of about fifty – shepherds, hut keepers, cooks, blacksmiths, fencers, bullock drivers and builders. This was a typical population on the existing stations.

In 1840, Monro was speared and came close to death. It happened the day after a clash, led by Cox of Darlington Station, in which an unknown number

Monro's Crossing. Henry Monro's ford is downstream from the old steel bridge on the Coliban River near Redesdale.

of Aboriginal men may have died. Monro foolishly rode his horse into a group of men carrying spears. One of the men threw a spear which hit Monro in the chest. Doctor Thomas, the leading doctor in Melbourne, was summoned and treated Monro successfully, praising the work of Monro's neighbour, Yaldwyn, who had treated the wound.

Monro was not prominent in public life. Apart from his clashes with Aborigines and squabbles with other settlers he did not make the news. He did not participate in the land speculation frenzy in Melbourne and apparently lived quietly on his station.

In 1843, Monro sold his run in two parts. The eastern part became Spring Plains Station and the western part Campaspe Station, now Coliban Park. He then purchased the 70,000 acre Crawford Station near Portland where he continued to lead a quiet life.

Henry Monro took his family to the UK and Europe in 1860. He died in Spain in 1869.

Captain John Hepburn

It is usually believed that John Hepburn and the Coghill brothers were the first to settle west of the Loddon River. We dispute this, as our ancestor, Abraham Braybrook, was one who definitely arrived at Maiden Hills, Burnbank in December 1837. Hepburn and the Coghills took up their stations in April 1838, four months later.

Hepburn had arrived in Sydney in 1835 as captain of the *Alice*. The owners sold the ship and left Hepburn in search of another position. He was made captain of the *Ceres*, trading between Sydney and the Hunter River. This proved too demanding for him and an acquaintance, John Gardiner, persuaded him to join him and Joseph Hawdon in a speculative drive with cattle to Port Phillip.

At Gundagai they met up with Granville Stapylton, the assistant surveyor from Major Mitchell's group, recently returned from

John Stuart Hepburn (1803–1860)

the exploration southwards. From him they received excellent advice concerning available land to the south.

The trip to Port Phillip was uneventful, but financially beneficial. The first person they met there was William Buckley and, soon after, John Batman. Buckley did not impress Hepburn who described him as 'a stupid fellow with no knowledge of the country.' He was to change his opinion drastically and later he described him as:

> 'The man who laid the foundation stone of this interesting colony. This I consider constituted the foundation of the capital of Victoria which has been lost sight of but is nevertheless true. He even made and laid a brick chimney for Batman.'

Buckley had lived with the Aborigines after he escaped from Captain Collins' failed attempt to establish a settlement at Portsea in 1803. His knowledge of the Aboriginal people was obviously superior to any other, having lived with them for thirty-two years.

With the cattle sold at a handsome profit, Hepburn, Gardiner and Hawdon returned to Sydney by ship.

Back in Sydney, Hepburn lost no time in teaming up with the Coghill brothers and setting out for the journey south, joining also with William Bowman, whom they met near Gundagai. They moved out in late 1837, taking an abundance of servants, prisoners of the crown, and a large number of sheep and cattle with them. Hepburn's objective was to locate the land Stapylton had told him about, of the 'valley of the finest description.' This they easily did.

John Hepburn was a good man who treated everyone with respect – he actually paid six of his ten convict servants thirty pounds a year each. This was indeed a rarity. He also appeared to have considerable regard for the Aboriginal people, and he had no clashes with them in all his experiences. He eventually employed some women in his household. He said at one time, 'the natives appeared to improve under the management of Mr Parker.' This was rare praise from a squatter, as most regarded Parker as just a 'do-gooder' who, in their opinion, interfered with their activities – as did all Protectors!

The magnificent house Hepburn built in 1849–50 is classified as 'of national importance, to be preserved at all costs'.

Henry Boucher Bowerman & William Allen

An early settler, generally overlooked, was Henry Boucher Bowerman. Like William Yaldwyn, Bowerman appointed an overseer, William Allen, to go forward with the stock, supplies and servants to select land in his name. Allen also chose well, selecting magnificent land in Mitchell's 'valley of the finest description', near modern-day Lexton. This is now the Mount Mitchell Station, somewhat of a national heritage treasure. The authors' ancestor, Abraham Braybrook, was one of the Allen party.

Bowerman was a well-off, retired military man with property on the Parramatta River where he grew fruit and vegetables. In November 1834, on the lookout for good men with farming experience, he selected Abraham Braybrook from the latest batch of convicts in the colony, fresh off the transport ship *Hooghly*.

Bowerman accumulated a good number of assigned men at Parramatta, far in excess of what was required. But he had plans that went beyond that scene – his intention was to become a big landholder.

When his friend Thomas Mitchell returned from his *Australia Felix* expedition, he told Bowerman of his 'valley of the finest description'. Bowerman decided to move in there as soon as he could make arrangements. He appointed 30-year-old William Allen as his overseer and quickly assembled stock and equipment at Yass. This included 7,000 sheep and 200 cattle, plus several carts, horses, bullocks, a boat, twenty-three convict servants and three free men. By 7th October 1837 they were ready to leave Yass.

Also ready to move were the parties of William Yaldwyn (headed by John Coppock while Yaldwyn remained in Sydney awaiting the birth of a child) and Captain Sylvester Brown.[10]

The Coppock/Yaldwyn group moved off first, followed two days later by Captain Brown. A further two days later, William Allen's party also headed for the 'promised land'. Allen had been instructed by Bowerman to select the land described in detail to him by Mitchell; he would follow in a couple of months in the comfort of a ship to Port Phillip.

---

10 Captain Brown was the father of Thomas Alexander Browne (he changed the spelling from Brown in the 1860s) who used the pen-name Rolf Boldrewood and wrote the Australian literary classic *Robbery Under Arms*.

By the end of November, the Bowerman party had reached the Goulburn River where they were a little surprised to be met by John Coppock who, unknown to them, had gone well ahead alone, made his selection for Yaldwyn, and promptly returned to meet up with his group. Coppock was a good bushman and was able to assist Allen on several river crossings and *vice versa* – Allen's boat was used a number of times for difficult river crossings.

Following the Major's Line, Allen eventually moved through Expedition Pass and what is now Castlemaine. By coincidence, they passed within 200 metres of our home in Bowden Street, Castlemaine. The journey was without serious incident, and the group arrived at their destination on 9th December 1837. Our family has pride in the fact that our ancestor Abraham was one of the first white men west of the Loddon River. Allen quickly set about exploring the area and laid claim to several thousand acres. As there were yet no other claimants, he had the choice of the best land.

Mount Kooroocheang.

It was definitely a wonderful selection of land by Allen; below the Pyrenees and well watered by several streams – Doctors, Burnbank and Bet Bet Creeks. The towering Mount Mitchell and the chain of Mammeloid Hills, Kooroocheang and Moorakile among them, were nearby.

Allen immediately put the men to work, and within a week a small village had sprung up on the bank of Mammeloid Creek. There was a three-roomed hut for the overseer, four small huts for the men and a couple of sheds.

The hut constructed for William Allen would have been typical of a squatter's accommodation – three rooms constructed of timber slabs with a bark roof and a dirt floor. One room was a storeroom for foodstuff, the second room was a spare. The main room of this rough hut served as a kitchen, dining room and bedroom with a rough bed, possibly with a possum skin cover. Other furniture consisted of several rough stools, possibly a large sea chest and a rough-hewn table. A large fireplace took up one entire end of the building. On the wall hung whips, guns, hobbles, dishes and sometimes a looking glass. A window, maybe only a foot square, was cut in one wall. On the table, several tin pannikins, tin plates and an old tin or jar filled with mutton fat with a bit of an old cloth as a wick, to provide light.

The less fortunate shepherds and other workers had no such luxuries, a canvas tent, a rough bed, and their cooking was done at an outdoor fireplace. The lucky ones had a small wattle and daub hut.

Bowerman arrived on horseback a week later, accompanied by two troopers for protection. His friend Captain Lonsdale had arranged this.

Henry Bowerman was delighted with Allen's choice and no doubt regarded his annual rent of ten pounds as money well spent! A week later, he returned to Port Philip and boarded a ship bound for Sydney.

He visited Maiden Hills again in February 1839 when checking on his several land investments in Melbourne (named by Governor Bourke in 1837). It was a quick visit to Maiden Hills, and then he returned to Sydney.

Meanwhile, Abraham Braybrook, John Davis and a lad named Denis Brennan were sent to set up an outstation on Mammeloid Creek and tend two thousand sheep. They chose a picturesque spot beneath an ancient red gum, beside a delightful, permanent waterhole. Their accommodation consisted of two heavy canvas tents sparsely set up with homemade furnishings.

They had occupied what proved to be a site frequented by the local Aboriginal people. Happily, the white interlopers soon became quite friendly with them. They exchanged meat and flour for murnong and the abundant fish and freshwater mussels. Davis even cut the men's hair, much to the delight of the women.

Bowerman had meanwhile acquired some land on the Plenty River, along with several blocks of land in Melbourne, intending to expand his farming interests. On 9th November 1839, after again briefly visiting Maiden Hills, he was a passenger on the ship *Britannia* bound for Sydney. He intended to share Christmas with his wife and family. The ship vanished without a trace. Henry Bowerman, along with the ship's crew and the rest of the passengers, was never seen again.

Although Bowerman is credited as being the first settler in the district, in reality the honour is with William Allen, three free men and his convict servants. Bowerman was rarely present on the run and did not actually select the land. Not long before his death, the Learmonth brothers had purchased his spread, which gave them land that extended from Buninyong to Burnbank, a distance of thirty miles. Bowerman had intended to focus on the rich farming and timber land of the Plenty River area. He died a very wealthy man.

In a short time the Learmonth brothers sold the northern half of the Maiden Hills run to Doctor Griffen. Hence the Mammeloid Creek became Doctor's Creek. In the painting of the Squatter's First Home by AD Lang, the man seated at the fire is believed to be Doctor Griffen.

Life in the Bush: The squatters first home, *AD Lang, 1847.*

William and George Faithfull

Though they did not settle in our district, it would be remiss not to write a little of these two brothers. In 1828, the brothers were each granted 640 acres of fine land on the Goulburn plains where William established Springfield. In 1838, with the area in drought, the brothers decided to overland to Port Phillip with a large number of sheep and cattle, along with about twenty convict servants, looking for other land. William decided to stay at Springfield.

On the way south, at the Ovens River, George had a look around at what land was available. He sent eighteen men ahead, droving a good part of the stock, with instructions to wait for him down the track. The men set up camp at the Broken River (present day Benalla). It seems that the travellers had been involved in an earlier dispute with Aborigines at the Ovens River where it is believed some tribesmen speared two cattle and that the men may have responded by shooting two of them dead. No proof exists of this, but it may explain the killings at what was to become known as the Faithfull Creek Massacre.

William Pitt Faithfull (1806–1889)

George Faithfull (1814–1855)

There is no certainty about what occurred at the Broken River, but we do know that at least eight shepherds were killed, more likely twelve or thirteen, and 'some' Aboriginal people also died. Because of the secrecy surrounding it, because there was the likelihood that men would be hanged if found guilty of murdering Aboriginal people, it is not possible to be sure what happened. The most likely cause of the attack was retaliation for the earlier incident at the Ovens River. George Faithfull always denied that this event had ever occurred.

Whatever the cause, it was a tragedy for the people concerned, black and white. Chief Protector George Robinson expressed his belief in the retaliation scenario, noting that Faithfull 'had several collisions with the natives that may have been found to be fatal.' Faithfull responded by claiming that Robinson used 'contemptible methods to gain information.' It was widely suggested that Faithfull lied to protect his men from hanging. He claimed that 200–300 Aboriginal warriors were involved, but it seems likely it was about 20. By claiming to be so outnumbered, it was justification for shooting Aboriginal men – self defence.

On reading George Faithfull's 1853 letter to Governor Latrobe, I formed the opinion that he was always belligerent toward all Aborigines. He actually stated, in writing, of another clash with the Aboriginal people, that he 'gave them a notion of what stuff white men are made of and my name was a terror for them forever after.' Of that clash he said, 'I trust and believe that many of the bravest savage warriors bit the dust.'

In any event, the massacre was sufficient for George to return northwards, where he established Bontharambo on Oxley Plains (Wangarattta). He claimed that he was constantly harassed by Aborigines, which forced him to move on in a matter of months. The property

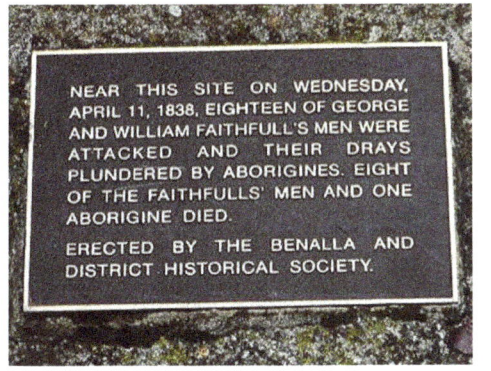

From: twistedhistory.net.au

was taken over by Reverend Joseph Docker who, oddly enough, had no difficulty whatsoever with the original inhabitants. It seems likely, therefore, that Faithfull continued to be deliberately at war with the Aboriginal people.

George Faithfull moved on to find greener pastures on the Ovens River. His brother William stayed on at Springfield, ultimately gaining much more property. He died a wealthy man with an estate of three hundred and fifty thousand pounds. George did pretty well, too.

***

There are many early settlers whose names live on: Hutton, Wedge, Yuille and Henty for example. William Yuille settled in the Ballarat district, as did the Learmonths originally.

Thomas and Somerville Learmonth began in April 1837 with 3,000 ewes, choosing land on each side of the Barwon River, about twenty miles from present day Geelong. In August 1837, they joined a party of six on an exploratory journey inland. They fancied Lake Burrumbeet and proceeded as far as Mount Elephant, which Thomas Learmonth named. In February 1838, the Learmonths moved to Buninyong.

The Learmonths estimated that 300 Aborigines lived in the Ballarat region. Thomas once stated that he had never killed one, even though they had murdered one of his servants. He also spoke of the 'disappearance of the indigenous people due to idleness, free food, and disease. Considering the wrong done to them – deprived of their country – they showed less ferocity and desire for retaliation than could be expected.'[11]

---

11 AGL Shaw 2003, A *History of the Port Phillip District: Victoria Before Separation*, Melbourne University Press.

The Learmonths later purchased Bowerman's Maiden Hills run and later still sold the northern half of that to Doctor Griffen. The two Scots are best remembered for Ercildoune, now heritage listed as a national treasure. They prospered and in 1855 purchased a further 26,000 acres for a massive seventy-five thousand pounds.

Looking for more investments, they bought the Mount Edgerton Mine in 1863. By 1873 the mine was not profitable. It appeared the gold had petered out, so they sold it at a bargain price to a speculator. Almost immediately the mine prospered once more. The brothers were furious to learn that the new part-owner of the mine was none other than their previous mine manager, the one who had presided over the losses and had advised them to sell. There followed a series of legal events, culminating in the Privy Council, in London, at that time Australia's top court. They spent eighty thousand pounds only to lose the case. Broken in spirit, they sold up and returned to live out their days in Scotland.

Thomas Learmonth 1818–1903

William Cross Yuille remained in Ballarat. (Lake Wendouree is actually Yuille's Swamp, a name present day residents would probably not find to their liking.)

Charles Wedge, in 1836, with his father John and brothers Edward and John, set up a station on the Werribee river. Tragedy struck in 1853 when the river flooded. The house was washed away and with it Edward, his wife and his daughter, who all drowned. Charles's brother, John junior, established a station at the Grange (Hamilton). There is a Wedge Street in Kyneton, which may be associated with the family.

> years.
> Drowned on Friday, 21st May, by the overflowing of the River Werribee, Edward Davy Wedge, Esq aged 76 years; Lucy, his wife, aged 64 years; and Lucy, their daughter. Universally respected by all who knew them.

The Henty family

When Major Thomas Mitchell arrived on the coast of south-west Victoria in August 1836, he was astonished to come upon what was obviously an established settlement of white people. Watching from a distance, he ordered his men to arm themselves, fearing it might be a camp of bushrangers or escaped convicts. Observing Mitchell and his crew from their homestead, the Hentys feared the same. Finally, each decided that the other was peaceful and Mitchell was warmly welcomed.

How and why had the Henty family arrived at this place? Seventy-year-old Thomas Henty was a well-off Sussex farmer and the father of seven sons. Looking for a good future for his boys, in 1833 he sold his farm for ten thousand pounds, a large fortune. He then migrated with his family to Western Australia. Dissatisfied with the prospects there, he moved to Launceston in Van Diemen's Land.

Edward Henty then explored the coast of the mainland for further opportunities. He came across Portland Bay, a deep port where William Dutton had run a whaling station since 1832, and was regularly used by a number of sealers.

Edward was pleasantly surprised to find the land about was ideal for grazing. He returned to Launceston and gathered up a good quantity of livestock and shipped it to the port in 1834. He was soon joined by others of the family, and a small village resulted.

Edward Henty 1810–1878.

The brothers established a whaling station in 1836 and operated that successfully, but their main interest was pastoral. Also in 1836, Stephen Henty purchased a small ship, the *Sally Ann*, and with numerous sheep and several assigned workers moved his home to Portland Bay. In the same year, Edward married in Van Dieman's land and brought his bride to live at Portland as well. Imagine how brave this young woman must have been. This was an extremely isolated place and the group was entirely dependent on themselves for food, health, protection from Aborigines and escaped convicts (real or imagined).

Thomas Mitchell told them of the good quality grazing land further inland and, before long, the family members occupied Mount Eckersley and by 1837 also held Merino Downs. By 1840, the Henty family had claimed an impressive six stations. Good news travels fast and by 1838 a good number of families had arrived at Portland, taking up huge areas of land around the district.

The Henty's even moved across the border into South Australia and occupied land there. It is recorded that on one of his exploratory trips, Stephen was the first white person to see the remarkable Blue Lake at Mount Gambier.[12]

There is not much detail available about relations with the local Aboriginals, but in 1853 Stephen Henty wrote that 'many of my men's lives were sacrificed to natives.' Who, where or how many was not revealed.

Joseph Tice Gellibrand

Gellibrand was not strictly among the early settlers of Port Phillip but he is an important man in its history.

Gellibrand was the first attorney general in Tasmania, appointed in 1824, with the right to practice as a barrister. This was at the same time as Sir George Arthur was appointed as Lieutenant-Governor. Unlike Arthur, Gellibrand was a liberal person and therefore not popular with Arthur. There was no friendliness between them, and Arthur did all he could to hinder and frustrate the Attorney General. The principal reason for the disagreement was Gellibrand's attempts to establish trial by jury, which Arthur used his power to withhold.

Joseph Tice Gellibrand (1786–1837)

In 1827, Gellibrand applied for a land grant, but was not successful, which was unusual for a man in his position. Without foundation, I suspect that Arthur was involved. In any event, the Governor eventually found a reason to

---

12 This distinctive and picturesque lake is set in an extinct volcano, with an average depth of over 70 metres and is now a major tourist attraction.

sack his attorney general, accused of unprofessional conduct. Arthur considered that Gellibrand was supplying Robert Murray, the editor of the *Hobart Town Gazette*, with inside information about him, which Murray was then using.

Gellibrand then took up a private law practice in Hobart and became a leading member of the Port Phillip Association, along with Batman and Fawkner. He made a number of visits to Port Phillip and, on one occasion, met a group of local Aboriginal people with John Batman. They were friendly. Batman presented the group with mirrors, knives, scissors and blankets. Then, through their interpreter, William Buckley, the men approved a treaty and land grant with John Batman, signing two documents prepared by Gellibrand. The papers stated that the 'Chiefs' granted Batman their surrounding territory with 'livery of seisin'.[13] Batman said that: 'They gave their own private marks which is sacred to them, even so much that women are not allowed to see them.'

> **GOVERNMENT ORDER.**
> Secretary's Office, Hobart Town,
> February 8, 1826.
>
> THE LIEUTENANT GOVERNOR has been under the Necessity of Suspending JOSEPH TICE GELLIBRAND, Esq. from the Office of Attorney General. JOSEPH HONE, Esq. Barrister at Law, is appointed Attorney General until His Majesty's Pleasure shall be known.
> By His Excellency's Command,
> JOHN MONTAGU, Secretary.
>
> ---
>
> **In the Press,**
> And will be published on Wednesday next, at the Office of the Colonial Times,
> PRICE, TWO DOLLARS.
>
> THE whole of the Proceedings in the Case of the Attorney-General, as well in the Supreme Court as upon the late private Investigation, including the Correspondence with His Excellency the Lieutenant Governor, His Honor the Chief Justice, and all the other Papers and Documents connected with this most important case.—Persons wishing Copies will please to signify the same to the Publisher, Mr. BENT, as only a limited Number will be printed.
>
> ---
>
> **POSTSCRIPT.**
> We exceedingly regret to have to announce, that yesterday morning it was the pleasure of His Excellency the Lieutenant Governor to suspend JOSEPH TICE GELLIBRAND, Esq. from the office of Attorney-General of this Island, to which he was appointed by His Majesty. JOSEPH HONE, Esq. Master of the Supreme Court, is to act as Attorney-General, until the pleasure of His Majesty is known.

He did not explain how these totally uneducated people, who spoke no English, knew what 'livery of seisin' meant. Batman also said that the men actually put their marks alongside the names he wrote on the document; Jagajaga, Cooloolook and Mammarmalar. More likely these are sounds

---

13 Livery of seisin is an archaic legal conveyancing ceremony used to convey holdings in property. It was practised in feudal England and other countries that followed English common law. (Wikipedia).

they uttered in answer to questions they did not understand. It is almost certain that the marks were made by Batman himself.

At that time Joseph Gellibrand, without having legal standing, appointed William Buckley official Superintendent of Native Tribes.

Joseph Gellibrand's memorandum, held in the State Library of Victoria, gives an important description of Melbourne and the surrounding district of 1836. He spent a month exploring the region and making notes of what he saw. He also journeyed to Indented Head (Geelong) where he witnessed Buckley being greeted with tears of joy by the local Aboriginal people. This proved to him the affection they had for the man.

His memorandum includes a description of the Aboriginal people as:

> A fine race of men, many handsome and well made. Very intelligent, strong teeth.
> ... The women, especially the young, are very modest in behaviour and dress. ... They all appear to be well disposed, and very fond of bread and potatoes. In the winter season they live principally on fish and game. Upon the appearance of the country, I feel persuaded that they must exert themselves considerably in obtaining subsistence, and from their extreme partiality to bread and potatoes, I feel not the slightest doubt but that they may be all brought to habits of industry and civilization, when the mode of obtaining potatoes and wheat country is generally ... [something seems to have been lost here] ... open, flat, champaign country, with abundance of verdure, and well watered. It far exceeds my expectations, although I was prepared to expect something very superior. I consider the representations of Mr. Batman fully borne out...

Gellibrand visited the mainland again in 1837 with his friend Fred Hesse. The pair went on a horse ride to Port Henry near Geelong. Near the junction of the Leigh and the Barwon rivers they farewelled a group and set off on an exploration toward the Otway ranges. They were never seen alive again.

Recent research has shown that their bodies were found, buried, two months after they went missing. Gellibrand's body was positively identified by his son, with supporting evidence from his teeth. For many

Gellibrand Pier, Williamstown, during the final period of transition from sail to fully powered steam vessels. Barque Gladys is shown taking in a cargo of bagged wheat. State Library, Victoria.

years, there was the notion that their bodies were never found. It seems that this legend was deliberately fostered to be part of the 'romance of the pioneers'. Indigenous witnesses stated that after they became lost, Gellibrand was separated from Hesse who apparently died from starvation. Gellibrand then lived with a friendly tribe, but on an occasion when most of the men of the tribe were away, an attack was made by an outlaw group of Indigenous people who murdered Gellibrand. [14]

In Joseph Gellibrand's memory we have Point Gellibrand, Gellibrand Park and Gellibrand Pier at Williamstown. He was a fine man with absolute confidence in the future of the Port Philip settlement to be 'one of the most important colonies under the British Crown'.

Additional Notes and Other Stories by Glenn Braybrook

The arrival of the first Europeans in our district had a huge impact on the local clans. It is probable that the resident Aboriginal people already had knowledge of Europeans arriving in far-off Port Phillip Bay. They had trading ties with the clans from that district and had named the bay area Cadong which, according to the natives, is a large piece of water on the coast. Nevertheless, it must have been a huge shock to find Europeans arriving in their country in large numbers.

The intruders had strange animals with them. There were some that they rode on that were also used to pull wagons. In addition, there were other unusual animals – hundreds of cows and many thousands of sheep.

As soon as the sheep arrived, they set about cropping the valuable murnong, the tubers of which were the staple diet for the Aborigines. Men with guns began killing the kangaroo and chasing them with dogs that could run as fast as the kangaroos, bringing them down and killing them. This had a huge effect on the Indigenous people's traditional food supply. Conflicts arose, not only about dwindling food supplies, but the trading of food – like sugar, meat, flour and tea – in exchange for the 'use' of Aboriginal women.

---

14 Donovan, Michael F, Ian D Clark and Fred Cahir, *The Remarkable Disappearance of Messrs Gellibrand and Hesse. What Really Happened in 1837? A Re-examination of the Historical Evidence.* Victorian Historical Journal, Vol 87, No 2, December 2016, p. 278.

One very sad and violent massacre came about for yet another reason. Some would never want it told, but it actually happened, so the story should be told. It was told to me some years ago by the late Alistair Clarke senior, the owner of Glengower Station at Campbelltown, south-west of Newstead.

My father and his brothers worked at Glengower in the 1950s when they were contract shearing and wool pressing. Their names can still be seen inside the ancient shearing shed at Glengower, along with hundreds of others, some dating back to the 1870s. They had stencilled them on the walls, bragging about how many bales they had pressed and how many sheep they had shorn and even how many beers they drank at the Black Duck Hotel, which still stands opposite the Glengower Station today.

Although named for a Scottish location, Glengower turns out to be an appropriate name for this station as Glen is a Scottish valley and Gauwa happens to be Dja Dja Wurrung for mountain or large hill. The station is in a valley with Deep Creek (or Joyces Creek) nearby and the huge volcanic mountains of Kooroocheang and Moorookile directly to the south.

Mr Clarke's story comes from 1840. There are a few variations of it, one comes from Edgar Morrison's 1960s books about the Loddon Aboriginal people, but I have chosen Alistair Clarke's version.

In 1840, Glengower Station was occupied by a Scottish sea captain, Dugald McLachlan. The station was surrounded by fellow Scots to the south, with Captain Hepburn at Smeaton Hill and Donald Cameron at the Clunes, where the first official paying goldfield was later found.

One day, a passing group of Aboriginal men were returning from Mount William (near present day Lancefield) to their country in the Grampians. They carried a supply of Greenstone, which was used to fashion their stone axes. They called into the station and found only the cook at work, the rest of the men were out preparing the sheep for the spring shearing.

What then took place between the Aborigines and the cook is hard to say, one story says the Aborigines were given flour with added plaster. This would solidify once eaten, causing a painful death. Another story is the cook refused them food and was murdered for his refusal. Either way, on returning from the day's work with the sheep, the cook was found dead, terribly mutilated, hanging from the meat hooks where the station's supply of mutton was kept. The stored mutton was taken away.

McLachlan was noted for his very bad temper and mean streak. He was furious and quickly assembled a number of men mounted on horses and armed with guns, and went after the Aborigines. They found them a few miles to the west of the station at a waterhole in the creek known as Middle Creek. On seeing the men on horses coming towards them, the Aboriginal people jumped into the waterhole; some found the reeds in the creek were hollow and they breathed through them. The men rode up and began shooting until every Aboriginal person was dead. It is not known how many

Glengower homestead. Photo courtesy National Trust of Australia.

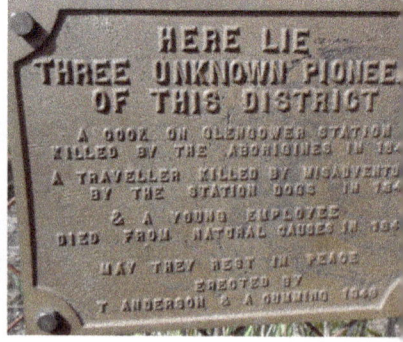

The plaque on the gravesite reads:
HERE LIE
THREE UNKNOWN PIONEERS
OF THIS DISTRICT
A cook on Glengower station
Killed by the Aborigines in 1840
A traveller killed by misadventure by the station dogs in 1841
& a young employee
Died from natural causes in 1841
May they rest in peace
Erected by
T Anderson & A Cumming 1949

(Left) The Glengower Pioneers Memorial Grave

were slain, but it was a significant number. The waterhole where this massacre took place has become forever known as the Blood Hole.

Over the years the location of this dark place had been forgotten, but not by Alistair Clarke, who told me exactly where it was. I realised that I had already visited the spot with historian John Tully, who had located it a few years before, but I didn't fully appreciate it at that time. The hollow reeds, which the Aboriginal people used as snorkels in 1840, still grow along the banks of the Blood Hole.

Following this incident, McLachlan purchased several fierce dogs which he chained up during the day and set free at night. The objective was to deter any Aboriginal people who may decide to visit or do harm. After dark one night there was a hell of a commotion in the yard. It was thought that the dogs warned off some intruders. Next morning the men were horrified to find a man's badly mauled body. He had apparently called on some errand and was attacked by the dogs. He was buried, without a name, alongside the unfortunate cook, some distance from the homestead. At about the same time, a young shepherd died from natural causes and he too was buried with the other two. The graves are marked by a small memorial erected by two caring local citizens more than a century later. There are no names attached to the monument.

The Aboriginal Protector

In 1840, Edward Stone Parker was appointed as one of the Assistant Protectors of Aborigines by Chief Protector George Augustus Robinson. Two others were appointed in other districts, but our concern is confined to the Loddon area. Parker saw the need to establish a permanent settlement for Indigenous people in a central location above the Loddon River.

Early in 1840, Robinson and Parker had travelled through the district, principally to examine allegations of the murder and mistreatment of local Aboriginal people. They were convinced of the truth of the allegations, but their reports were generally swept under the carpet. At the same time, they were scouting for a suitable site for a protectorate.

Parker was a dedicated and caring man, sincere in his endeavours to help the Original people. He complained particularly of 'the pernicious intercourse they have with the vitiated portion of the lower classes'. Seemingly, he overlooked the fact that many of the 'better' class also had pernicious relations with Aboriginal people, particularly the women.

In September 1840, Parker assembled all the men and equipment he could muster and set off to the Loddon district to establish the protectorate. His choice of land was on the banks of the Loddon at Mackinnons' Station (later to become known as Tarringower, Plaistow and Rodborough Vale[15]). Three Mackinnon cousins had taken up a total of about 95,000 acres there. I have no record of the squatters' feelings about this, but I imagine they were not positive.

Edward Stone Parker (1802–1865), Aboriginal Protector, Franklinford Aboriginal Station.

The area he chose is still known today as Parkers Plains, with the chosen head station about a mile upstream from Neereman, now known as Hamiltons Crossing. These days Hamiltons Crossing is a very pleasant, relatively unknown, camping and fishing spot.

By November, forty-one members of the Dja Dja Wurrung had arrived, 'destitute of clothing', ordered away from their hunting grounds by the white intruders. They had met Parker previously and had high regard for him, in fact they called him Marmingorak, meaning 'Father of all'.

As the year moved into summer, and a particularly hot and dry summer, it soon became apparent that the area was not suited to the needs of the Protectorate. Parker sent his overseer Blazely on an excursion to find a better place. Blazely chose a site below Mount Franklin. This was an outstation on the run of Andrew Mollison who offered no objection.

George Augustus Robinson inspected the area and found it suitable and he spoke highly of it to Latrobe. Actually, his first choice was nearby at Strangways, but strong objection from squatter MacKinnon put an end to that. Lyon Campbell, not to be confused with William Campbell of Strathloddon, also objected, but he, apparently, was ignored.

---

15 Edward Gittins purchased from Donald Mackinnon 1,000 sheep and the property of 23,400 acres (9470 hectares) for £250. He named the property Rodborough Vale, after Fort Rodborough in Gloucestershire.

Edward Stone Parker, Aboriginal Protector, member of Legislative Council..

Acting on Robinson's recommendation, Lieutenant-Governor Latrobe sent Surveyor Powlett to map the place, and in June 1841, Parker moved from Neereman. By 18th June, over one hundred and twenty Aboriginal people had already arrived. Between July and August, thirty-five acres had been fenced, and thirteen acres were ready for cultivation. Five acres were planted with wheat, and a temporary house, a store and three good huts were completed.

Parker's close contact with these people was a learning experience for him. He was impressed with the free and easy ways of the people: They were 'carefree and lived the moment'. However, some of their practices shocked him. For example, he was horrified to learn that an Aboriginal woman had killed her one-day-old baby. This, he was told, was the third time. Her reason was that she was afraid she would become old and wrinkled and less desirable to men. True or false, Parker apparently believed it. On the other hand, women displayed strong maternal feeling. The men often showed strong affection to their woman.

He also learned firsthand of the belief that nobody died naturally but that death was usually the result of some act by a member of another group. The clan would eagerly seek an opportunity for revenge.

A highlight for the settlement was the visit of the recently replaced Lieutenant-Governor of Tasmania, Sir John Franklin, and his wife, on 23rd December 1843. The couple and their entourage were making their way to be with Captain and Mrs Hepburn at Smeaton Hill for Christmas Day. The Franklins had paused in their return journey to England to visit an old friend.

The couple enjoyed roughing it and camped under the stars, beneath their cart. Before calling on Parker, they had ascended the nearby mountain, known by the settlers as Jim Crow Hill and by the Aboriginal people as Lalgambook.

They stayed fifty hours at the settlement before crossing the Jim Crow Creek via a ford below the settlement. Forever after it became known as Franklin Ford and the mountain became Mount Franklin.

How did the creek become named Jim Crow? There is no certainty and there are a few stories. In his writings, Edgar Morrison tells the tale that it was named by Captain Hepburn. Morrison said that as he and a companion rode through the area, Hepburn's friend said, 'What do you think we should call these hills?' Hepburn is said to have replied, 'Call them Jim Crow.' Why he would have chosen that is not known, but it is also possible, as Morrison writes, that he used the name taken from a popular song of the time which contained the words 'Hop a little, skip a little, jump Jim Crow.' This may have been running through his head at the time.

Another theory is that the Aboriginal name for the creek was Jem Cra, or similar, which easily became Jim Crow. The hill was named Lalgambook and it may have been that the creek also had that name. Nobody will ever know, but it remains Jim Crow Creek, in spite of some suggestions it may be derogatory to Aboriginals! A small group currently demands a change of name. Maybe the change is deemed necessary because African slaves in America were often called 'Jim Crows'; but what does that have to do with Jim Crow Creek in Australia? In any event, 'Jim Crow' has been there since 1838 and is part of Australia's heritage and history.

A group of Aboriginal men, women and children standing in front of a slab hut on ES Parker's farm. Picture: Richard Daintree and Antoine Fauchery c1857, SLV.

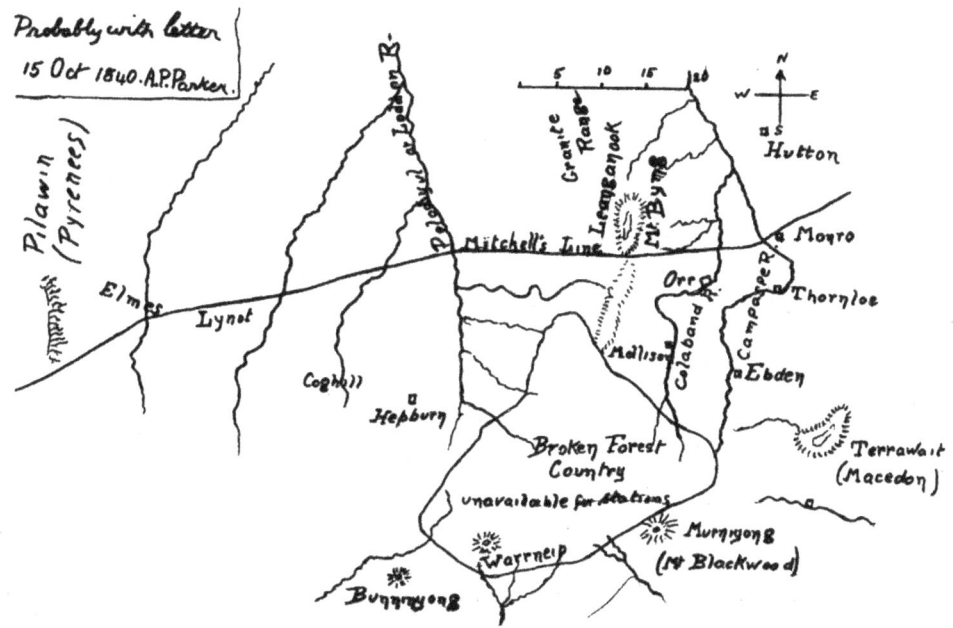

Mr Parker's Sketch Map of March 1840 From: Barry Golding: barrygoanna.com/beyond-contact (after Morrison, 1966) retrieved 19/08/2019.

In his report to the Governor in 1845, Chief Protector George Robinson expressed his pleasure with the success of Franklinford. Of his visit he wrote: 'About 100 Aboriginals congregated at the station, many of them engaged in bringing in the harvest and other useful labour. There are two drivers, two shepherds and two domestics.' The workers were even being paid a small wage and they were 'shown a kind attitude,' There can be little doubt that the Protectorate was a success, but at Government House, enthusiasm for protection in general was on the wane, and they were seeking ways of abandoning the project with honour.

In 1848, Parker learned another lesson in Aboriginal people's behaviour. To his alarm, almost overnight, the settlement was abandoned by all but a couple of the families. There was no obvious reason. Two months later, with no explanation offered, they all reappeared. Was this Parker's first taste of the habit of Aboriginal people's walkabout?

Dry conditions prevailed again in 1848, and Parker's station was plagued with cattle from neighbouring properties straying onto his good grasses. The main offender was William Hunter of Tarrengower. Parker tried to make peace with Hunter, without success. Much damage to the viability of the protectorate resulted.

The Franklin Ford at Jim Crow Creek.

This provided an opportunity for the government, and the Protectorate was shut down, effective from early 1850. Parker was upset with the decision, but had no alternative than to accept it. He was, after all, a man of excellent character who really cared, and he tried his utmost to protect his charges from the worst characteristics of white men.

As compensation, he was granted a lease of 66 acres and proceeded to set up a new homestead below the mountain. In 1853 he was chosen as a member of the Legislative Council and was later appointed as inspector of schools for the Goldfields District. He continued to care and provide shelter for the Indigenous people until his death in 1865 aged 57. His grave at Franklinford cemetery is marked by a large monument atop a family plot. The plot contains the remains of a number of his family and descendants.

Two items deserve mention. At midnight on 11th October 1842, his first wife died without warning while he was absent in Melbourne. At two o'clock in the morning, a young convict shepherd rode hell for leather the eighty miles over barely formed tracks, on a very dark night, to fetch Parker. Eventually locating Parker, he rode home with his master and arrived at nine o'clock in the evening of that same day. What a feat of devotion by convict lad John McLoughlin.

Also of interest is that Parker wrote in his last report of 1851 that in 1849 a young Aboriginal lad picked up a stone to throw at a bird. It was, in fact, a gold nugget which a fellow shepherd took from him and kept secret for two years. If this is true, the squatters owed him a great debt. Their tranquil, trouble free existence was extended by two years until the great finds of 1851.

1. Franklinford monument.
2. Aboriginal protector, Edward Stone Parker's 66 acre farm below Mount Franklin c1858. Richard Daintree and Antoine Fauchery. SLV.
3. Grave of Edward Stone Parker at Franklinford cemetery.
4. Aboriginal farm workers at Franklinford 1858. Picture, SLV.

Part Three

Gold

Charles Joseph Latrobe

Charles Joseph Latrobe (Joe to the diggers), Superintendent of Port Phillip from 1839 and then Lieutenant-Governor from 1851 to 1854, was the first government official appointed to the Port Phillip District. He was English-born into a well-off family and educated at an exclusive school in Switzerland. This may explain why he didn't understand the feelings of the ordinary people he governed, the gold seekers on our goldfields. He was a cultured gentleman with no military, administrative or political experience and was a really bad choice for the role of lieutenant-governor. Although he had extensive powers as superintendent until January 1851, he was ultimately answerable to Governor Gipps in Sydney.

In 1850, the home government in London, finally responding to loud demands, changed the Colonial Government Act to give Port Phillip its own government. This raised Latrobe's position from Superintendent to Lieutenant-Governor.

From day one of his upgraded appointment, he had an economy that was seriously under-resourced with limited income-raising powers.

Charles Joseph Latrobe (1801–1875)

When gold was discovered in NSW by Hargraves early in 1851, Latrobe's problems increased dramatically. There was trouble looming.

Latrobe's house.

When gold was eventually discovered in the Port Philip District, Latrobe enforced the collection of a monthly license fee from the diggers, who regarded the fee as a tax. The tax bore no relationship to the diggers' ability to pay. Latrobe's gold commissioners, backed by armed force, collected the tax with sometimes excessive vigour. These administrative decisions were serious mistakes, and Latrobe was ultimately forced into a humiliating backdown.

Under constant pressure, Latrobe finally tendered his resignation in 1852. The wheels turned slowly and it was not until March 1854 that his replacement, Charles Hotham, arrived in Melbourne.

In the interim, Latrobe had been hit with the sad news that his wife had died in Switzerland. When he was back home in England, he was tragically stricken with an eye complaint that cost him his sight. Totally blind, he was unable to write his planned book on the experiences of a colonial governor. To his everlasting credit, before he died he returned all of his notes, documents and letters to the people of Victoria where they are now available for us to see in the State Library.

Tons of Gold

In 1851, the colony of Victoria consisted of about 25,000 people in Melbourne and 8,000 in Geelong. There was a scattering of perhaps 1,000 leaseholders across the outlying districts, the squatters were paying a pittance for the use of vast acres of public land – or should we say Aboriginal people's land. They were paying, in total, rent of twenty thousand pounds for approximately sixty million acres.

The government was controlled by men (of course, no women allowed) who were landholders, business and professional men selected

THE SYDNEY GOLD DIGGINGS.

The *Sydney Herald* of the 23rd May, two days later, has been received overland. The following is therefore the latest intelligence from the diggings. Our readers will see that Sir C. Fitzroy has interfered by a proclamation What a queer donkey our new Governor-General must be to meddle in an affair where his autho.ity is certain to be laughed at :—

THE GOLD MINE.—We have been favoured by a gentleman who returned from the Ophir mines yesterday with the following outline of his excursion, which cannot fail in greatly interesting our readers :—Left Sydney on Friday night by mail ; arrived late on Saturday at Bathurst ; hired horse and proceeded to Mrs Lister's inn, Guyong district twenty-three miles distant from Bathurst ; fell in with Mr Hargraves, the discoverer, there, who kindly offered to accompany me at daybreak to the diggings at the

MONDAY MORNING, JUNE 2, 1851.

WE have heard a great deal about the " gold mania," and of the probable disastrous consequence which are to ensue from its propagation. But there is another disease which is just as prevalent, and which is every whit as dangerous. It is the " aurophobia." Those infected with the first named distemper, have an almost irresistable inclination to rush to the diggings, in the certainty of finding gold in half-pound lumps every hour of the day ; while the victims of the " aurophobia" wring their hands in dispair, cry out that all is lost—that the gold will be the ruin of the country—and that the future is shrouded in a mist of black despair.

GOLD IN NEW SOUTH WALES!

We have the following intelligence by private letter from New South Wales, under date of the 16th instant :—

" We are in a state of excitement at Sydney, second only to that of our trans-Pacific friends in California experienced two years ago, in the discovery of an El Dorado of our own thirty miles from Bathurst, and which is likely to prove not inferior to that. What is to be the result of course cannot be foreseen,but there is no mistake as to the fact of one piece being brought to Sydney nine and a half ounces weight, and numerous smaller ones. Fares to the regions are quadrupled by the coaches, 10*l* being now asked ; and large parties have gone from Bathurst. and many are going from here. Flour on Wednesday might have been bought below 20*l*, perhaps 19*l* or 18*l* 10s. This morning one party took forty tons at 20*l*—and during the day parties have been uttering the figures of 26*l* and 30*l* per ton. Horses, 30s to 50s, three days since at auction, re-sold at 10*l* to 14*l* per head. The drayman I employ

The right to all precious metals being vested in the Crown, the Governor had decided upon granting monthly licenses to the diggers, which from the following paragraph appears to have been well received.

(Top left) South Australian Gazette and Mining Journal, *14 June 1851. (Bottom left)* Geelong Advertiser, *2 Jun 1851, p 2. (Top right)* The Britannia and Trades' Advocate *(Hobart Town, Tas) 2 Jun 1851 p 3. (Bottom right)* The Perth Gazette and Independent Journal of Politics and News *(WA), 22 Aug 1851, p 3..*

by Lieutenant-Governor Latrobe. It was one of the most undemocratic governments in the world.

The newly independent colony was struggling. Poor management by Latrobe, who was inexperienced in administration, was a major cause of shortages in almost every sector of the government. The colony's future looked grim.

Things got worse in June 1851 when the government of NSW announced that there was gold to be had at Bathurst. The news precipitated a mass exodus of people from Victoria and was the last thing the government needed! Latrobe told his government that the colony must counter this by finding payable gold. If not found soon, the colony was doomed. Visions for the future of the colony would be nothing but an unfulfilled dream.

Men, women and children on their way to the diggings from Sydney, 1851.

The situation was dire, and a reward of two hundred and twenty pounds was offered to anyone finding payable quantities of the precious yellow metal.

Almost immediately there was a rush of claims, but regrettably, they proved to be false. Then came two genuine claims, one from a man at what is now Warrandyte and the other from James Edmunds at Clunes station, owned by squatter Donald Cameron.

The Warrandyte claim soon proved to be a shicer[1] and the one at Clunes was little better, although it was enough for Edmunds to successfully claim the reward; so he actually did pretty well out of it!

Things rapidly slowed down at Clunes, and within a month most diggers gave up in disgust. To Latrobe and his government it looked very much like the colony was ruined as the rush to NSW continued unabated.

Then, in answer to the government's prayers, salvation came in the form of Thomas Hiscock who hailed from the tiny timber harvesting settlement of Buninyong, near Yuille's Ballarat run.

---

1   An unproductive mine – a duffer.

Intrigued by James Edmund's find at Clunes, Hiscock began fossicking. In August he found gold! The word spread like wildfire, and in days Buninyong was inundated with gold seekers.

Some good finds were uncovered by a handful of diggers, but nothing too exciting.

> EXPLORATIONS.—Old stories are now taken as gospel truths, what heretofore was smiled at, now commands attention. The Pyrennees gold discovery has passed from the apocryphal to the canonical, and the doubter is becoming the convert. Several explorers in a body left for a locality within thirty miles of Geelong, brimful of confidence a few days ago. The Yow Yangs will be visited this week, and we should not be surprised to see a band of adventurous diggers establish themselves in the gully leading to Little Scotland. Wives had better keep a sharp eye on saucepan lids and frying pans, lest husbands and sons decamp therewith.

Meanwhile, 70-year-old John Dunlop and his young mate, James Reagan, were fossicking around the White Horse Range on Yuille's run at nearby Ballarat. On 21st August 1851 they found gold at the eastern end of the range – and lots of it. The duo worked in secret for several days and washed an unknown quantity of gold – probably many ounces – the first of an official twenty million ounces that would eventually be uncovered in Ballarat.

In the last days of August, Alfred Clarke, a reporter from the *Geelong Advertiser*, went for a ride. At the junction of the Yarrawee Creek and Yuille's Creek he noticed a discolouration of the water. He followed the Yarrawee and soon came upon the two diggers. Their secret was out. 'I would sooner have seen the Devil than him,' Reagan was later to say.

If ever there was a misnomer it was the one given to the area by the diggers. Poverty Point was anything but that. By mid-September, 2,500 men were working the creeks and embankments. The once pristine ground had the appearance of a devastated battleground, with piles of red and yellow clay in every direction. There were fantastic finds, unbelievable yields for the work of a single day – the Cavanagh brothers took 630 ounces, another party took 560 ounces and Brown's party harvested 314 ounces.

The official recorded total was 35,000 ounces in the first 3 months. The true total will never be known. Victoria might yet survive.

***

Often overlooked or ignored is the first serious gold find in the colony, at Daisy Hill, near present day Maryborough. In 1849, a young shepherd name Thomas Chapman uncovered what he was sure was gold. He promptly quit his job and carried his quite large prize to Melbourne.

> **MORE GOLD.**—A few days ago a bushman brought to the shop of Mr. Brentani, watchmaker in this city, a bag of dust, in which was found a small proportion of gold. The dust was gathered in the direction of the Pyrenees, about seventy miles from the "scene" of the "diggins" which some twelve months ago caused one half of Melbourne to lose its wits.—*Melbourne Morning Herald.*

According to a report in the *Cornwall Chronicle*, Launceston, 18th March 1849 he took his prize to Brentani, a wily jeweller in Collins Street for appraisal. One piece weighed twenty-four ounces and a second was fourteen ounces. Brentani declared it good quality gold and made an immediate purchase. He gave the lad a pair of trousers, five shirts and a coat, plus twenty pounds in cash. The second, smaller piece was bought by another jeweller named Duchene for eight pounds. Young Chapman was well satisfied, as it was more money than he had ever seen; a shepherd was lucky to be paid twenty pounds a year. He gave Brentani a good description of the locality where his find was made, but refused to take anyone there. He obviously had other things to do, now that he had heaps of cash!

Meanwhile, word had somehow spread and by the time Brentani and two friends arrived at the spot, there were several men working the land.

But not for very long! The squatter who leased the run, saw the activity and, in a state of alarm, immediately sent word to Latrobe. At that time, the last thing the squatters (and therefore the government) wanted was a gold rush. Such a thing would drain the workers from their employ and that spelt disaster. To protect the employers, the law decreed that any person even fossicking for gold would be severely dealt with. Under the Masters and Servants Act, an offender faced six months in jail, a flogging and confiscation of any wages due. This was, of course, to change when, in February 1851, Hargraves made his discovery in New South Wales, and up to a thousand men a day left Melbourne for the Bathurst diggings.

But at that time, Latrobe immediately dispatched an armed squad of troopers who promptly and thoroughly dispersed the assembled gold seekers. As they had found no encouraging traces, they left Daisy Hill without much protest, and it returned to its peaceful existence.

Relief for Latrobe

At the same time as the happenings at Ballarat, another scene was taking place in a gully beside a creek on Doctor William Barker's run, below Mount Alexander, about ninety kilometres to the north of Ballarat, and a few kilometres from Castlemaine.

Imagine the impact of the following letter published in the *Argus* on 8th September 1851.

> DEAR SIR.—I wish you to publish these few lines in your valuable paper, that the public may know that there is gold found in these ranges, about four miles from Doctor Barker's home station, and about a mile from the Melbourne road; at the southernmost point of Mount Alexander, where three men and myself are working. I do this to prevent parties from getting us into trouble, as we have been threatened to have the Constables fetched for being on the ground. If you will have the kindness to insert this in your paper, that we are prepared to pay anything that is just when the Commissioner in the name of the party comes.
> JOHN WORLEY.
> Mount Alexander Ranges,
> Sept. 1st, 1851.

John Worley was a free man, a bullock driver, who had brought his wife Bridget and their daughter from Goulburn in 1849 to work for Dr William Barker on his Mount Alexander station. He and his three mates, Christopher Peters, Robert Keen and George Robinson, had been secretly working the area since late July, when one of the men observed numerous pieces of gold embedded in quartz in an embankment. They had promptly resigned their jobs, telling Dr Barker they were leaving the district for other work.

John Worley and companions monumental cairn in Specimen Gully, Mount Alexander.

They didn't leave, but stayed on, digging up a fortune. When Barker came across them he was furious and ordered them off his land, threatening to have them prosecuted; hence the letter to the *Argus*. It seems that the well-off Dr Barker had no interest in gold and probably feared what a rush would mean to his farm workers.

The letter hit Melbourne like a bomb and almost at once a mass departure of its citizens began. Included in the rush to Forest Creek were many men from Ballarat, where the easily won gold had quickly become scarce.

Why was the discovery recorded for Forest Creek and not Mount Alexander where the Worley group made the discovery? Unsure of the actual site mentioned by Worley, the first two parties to arrive decided to try washing in a small creek just south of the mountain. To their great joy they found gold in abundance. Nuggets were clearly visible in the bed of the stream and on the creek banks and the surrounds. They were able to take gold from the water or the ground, requiring nothing more than a pick or a pocket knife to lever pieces of gold from where they lay.

This was an astounding discovery and quickly placed Forest Creek on the map, not only locally, but soon throughout the world. Those unnamed early arrivals gathered up huge wealth, the extent of which we will never know.

By the end of the first week of October, there were just the two parties sharing the wealth. By the end of the month, there were several hundred, and by the end of November there were 8,000. These diggers were feverishly working Forest Creek, Campbells Creek and Barkers Creek. They found gold in vast quantities, filling their pockets, billy cans, and saddle bags. Before long, it was estimated that 25,000 men were at work on the goldfield. By early 1852, there wasn't a flat or a gully left unpopulated. There was tent upon tent, almost one on top of the other, stretching all along Forest Creek to what is now Castlemaine. Scarcely a tree was left standing. There were similar scenes on every creek in the area.

Forest Creek rightly lays claim to be the richest shallow alluvial goldfield the world has ever seen. Today it is named Chewton. I have been informed it was renamed after a cheese making village in England. Why it did not remain Forest Creek, or why it has not reverted to its original name, is puzzling. Forest Creek was known throughout the world, but whoever has heard of Chewton? Reverting to the name Forest Creek would possibly carry more weight than Chewton in the eagerly sought after World Heritage listing.

Melbourne Town quickly became almost deserted. Men from all walks of life moved to Forest Creek – labourers, lawyers, doctors, public servants, even policemen, not to mention shepherds and farm workers. Of course, this added to Latrobe's woes. Instead of improving the situation, it became even worse as it was impossible to get employees. Latrobe was forced to offer large salaries, but even this had little effect.

At Forest Creek

The entire area resembled a giant graveyard. Forest Creek was a scene of utter devastation. The heat and the flies became almost unbearable and a drought was on the land. To add to the unpleasantness, there was a constant, overpowering stench filling the air. Discarded offal and unwanted meat were dumped in disused shafts by the several makeshift slaughterhouses. As well as that, there was the stink emanating from the many disused shafts used as lavatories. Disease flourished.

MOUNT ALEXANDER DIGGINGS.
(FROM OUR OWN CORRESPONDENT)
November 3rd, 1851.

My last was a hurried account of what I saw after a visit of a few hours, consequently it did not contain much interesting matter. Since that time, I have been both up and down the creek, and having time on hand, will make you acquainted with what information I have gleaned The diggings are not on Mount Alexander, as is generally supposed, but in a gully known as Forest Creek, and situated about seven miles from the Mount, and twenty from the Loddon, which receives the waters of this Creek. It is generally supposed that the gully contains gold the whole distance, and tents are being pitched for four miles lower down than the Commissioners. The sides of the ranges are covered

A diggers hole dug through 'cement', Forest Creek.

For the gold-seeker, it was a matter of pot luck – dig and hope. And the digging was hard, through dry dirt and gravel. It was not unusual for two men to dig for a day and finish up with a hole only a foot deep, or less.

For most it was a heartbreaking, backbreaking disappointment, but there was always the hope that the next hole would be a 'jewellers shop', the name the diggers gave to super-productive holes.

By February 1852, the Forest Creek district was a hot, foul-smelling dust bowl. The air was filled with dust as fine as talcum powder, as the heat continued. The creek refused to flow and what trickle there was, quickly turned to mud. With no water to wash the dirt, there was no gold. In desperation, some men pushed wheelbarrows full of dirt to the Loddon River fifteen kilometres away. A few who could afford it paid one of the several dray and wagon operators for the task. Others simply stockpiled their wash dirt in the hope of rain and a flow in the creek.

Then, in May, the drought broke – and in a big way. Torrential rain fell and what had been a sea of dust became a sea of mud. The persistent rain was driven by strong, freezing winds. Life became even more miserable.

By this time, large numbers of diggers had given up and returned to their jobs – at least until the conditions improved.

***

Surprisingly, there was very little crime on the goldfields even though there were few, if any, police to keep control. The diggers made their own laws and woe betide any man that violated them. In fact, there was

A shallow grave at Pennyweight Flat cemetery.

far less crime on the goldfields than in the towns.

Illness was widespread – influenza, colds, rheumatism and, worst of all, dysentery, which claimed many lives. Dotted throughout the area were small cemeteries, mostly containing unmarked graves. They were careful of course not to select ground that may be gold bearing!

The Pennyweight Flat Cemetery, commonly known as the Children's Cemetery, is still regularly visited and is well maintained. A look at the names recorded there gives a good indication of the origins of the general population. Names from Great Britain, Ireland, America, Scandinavia, Italy and France, and more. This was probably the foundation of Australia as a tolerant, multi-cultural land.

One name of interest to the authors is Anne Braybrook, age 31, buried there in 1853. Her weeks-old child predeceased her by about a week and may have been buried in the Barkers Creek cemetery, of which no trace or record can be found. Anne was the wife of George Braybrook, and is probably an ancestor, but we have not been able to confirm this. It appears that after his wife and child died he moved on to somewhere unknown.

We know that he signed the Red Ribbon Rebellion petition to Governor Latrobe in 1853, so he was still in the area then. His name cannot be found on shipping records to indicate that he left Australia.

The Pennyweight Flat Cemetery contains a disproportionate number of children, probably a hundred or more, although no truly reliable record appears to be available. Rowan McMillan[2] suggests that 200 children are buried there. It is located on a rocky slope where the ground is so tough that only very shallow graves were dug. Many of these unfortunate people, most commonly victims of dysentery, were wrapped in cloth or sometimes in sheets of bark for a shroud, and laid to rest two or three feet below the surface.

***

One lucky strike could set a man up for life, so the gold seekers were driven on. Above all, they enjoyed freedom from servitude to often harsh masters. On the goldfields, everyone was equal. Many an aristocratic type was seen to wince when addressed by a rough looking digger as 'mate'.[3]

Life was particularly hard for the women, especially if they had children to care for; living in a hot or leaky tent, cooking on an open fire and trying to keep bodies and clothing clean with whatever water was available. And if a husband died, as too often happened, how did they manage? They had little choice but to obtain work for a miserable pittance or, as some did, turn to prostitution. There was no other way.

We honour those wonderful women of the goldfields, indeed all of our pioneer women.

---

2 McMillan, AR 1988, The Pennyweight Kids: 1852–1857, AR McMillan.

3 In *Mateship: A Very Australian History*, Dr Nick Dyrenfurth traces the term 'mate' back to the very first white Australians – the convicts. 'The convicts brought with them from Britain the term mate, and they used it amongst themselves … 'They even rather provocatively termed their jailors mate and the basic message was "you're no better than us" … On the goldfields, they also referred to each other as mates ... as business partners. For them, mateship was about making a buck … To go mates with a fellow miner meant that you were friends with a fellow miner, but it also denoted a business partnership.' From *Aussie mateship: Tracing the history of a defining cultural term* by Margaret Burin, abc.net.au accessed September, 2019.

Forest Creek soon overshadowed the finds in New South Wales, and the exodus from Victoria went into reverse. Gold Commissioners were busily collecting the new thirty shillings a month licence fee that had been introduced by Latrobe in September 1851 following the finds at Ballarat.

From late December 1851 to mid-January 1852, six ships carried 8 tons of gold to England. When it was unloaded there, the impact was massive. The publicity was hard to ignore. People struggling to survive immediately wanted to go to the source and asked, 'How do we get there?'

The answer proved to be via the Assisted Passage Scheme, set up earlier with little success, intended to encourage growth in the colony's population. It certainly achieved that, albeit by means not predicted. Gold fever was on the rampage, as individuals and families queued for tickets. The rush from Great Britain was on!

On arrival at Melbourne these hope-filled migrants were ripped off at every opportunity, beginning with large fees to land their belongings onshore. Then they may be charged five shillings to sleep on a straw mattress on the floor of a shed, or, if they fancied a drink, two shillings for a glass of warm beer.

Mount Alexander from Saw Pit Gully (1856). Samuel Charles Brees, 1810–1865.

Over at Ballarat, Charles Latrobe was quick to see the opportunity for generating income for his depleted treasury by taking money from the gold discoveries. He promptly adopted the same license fee that was instituted by Fitzroy after the NSW finds, a law demanding a license fee of thirty shillings (one pound ten shillings) a month to look for gold.

Right from its enactment, there was sporadic debate over the apparent injustice of the licensing system, as it favoured the government and not the people who paid what was seen as a tax.

Within days of the proclamation, a squad of troopers, led by Commissioner Doveton, arrived at Buninyong. There they were met by hostile men who quickly organised a protest meeting. But there was no relenting from Doveton who proceeded to collect the fees. The diggers were no doubt intimidated by the presence of armed soldiers as backup to the Commissioner. A good number of men fled into the bush, as they had no capacity to pay the fee.

> **LICENSES TO DIG AND SEARCH FOR GOLD.**
> *(From a Supplement to Yesterday's Government Gazette.)*
>
> COLONIAL Secretary's Office, Sydney, 23rd May, 1851.—With reference to the Proclamation issued on the 22nd May, instant, declaring the rights of the Crown in respect to gold found in its natural place of deposit within the territory of New South Wales, His Excellency the Governor, with the advice of the Executive Council, has been pleased to establish the following provisional regulations, under which licenses may be obtained to dig, search for, and remove the same: —
>
> 1. From and after the first day of June next, no person will be permitted to dig, search for, or remove gold on or from any land, whether public or private, without first taking out and paying for a license in the form annexed.
>
> 2. For the present, and pending further proof of the extent of the gold field, the license fee has been fixed at one pound ten shillings per month, to be paid in advance; but it is to be understood that the rate is subject to future adjustment, as circumstances may render expedient.
>
> 3. The licenses can be obtained on the spot, from the Commissioner, who has been appointed by His Excellency the Governor to carry these regulations into effect, and who is authorised to receive the fee payable thereon.
>
> 4. No person will be eligible to obtain a license, or the renewal of a license, unless he shall produce a certificate of discharge from his last service, or prove to the satisfaction of the Commissioner that he is not a person improperly absent from hired service.
>
> 5. Rules adjusting the extent and position of land to be covered by each license and for
>
> *From the Sydney Morning Herald, 24 May 1851, p 2.*

Off to the diggings!

It was pretty easy to say that you were 'off to the diggings', but in practice it was far from easy. Getting from Melbourne to Ballarat was seventy miles of hard going via Geelong. It was about eighty miles to the new, and more promising, Forest Creek diggings, proceeding along the Mount Alexander Road, the name it still retains. In 1851 it was no more than a rough bush track leading north to the few settlements in the Swan Hill district, used by only a handful of squatters and the occasional hawker.

It took a day to get to Diggers Rest. In summer it was hot and dusty, in winter, cold and wet. If you were fortunate you had a horsedrawn cart, but more likely it was on foot, maybe pushing a wheelbarrow filled with your worldly goods. Day two would find you at the Bush Inn at Gisborne where you could quench your thirst with a hot beer at six shillings a bottle! On day three it was through the Black Forest to Carlsruhe and day four arrival at Forest Creek.

From then on it was pot luck, you either struck it rich or, like the vast majority, carved out a meagre living or even less. But there was hope!

The commissioners were kept busy with the numerous gold escorts conveying the riches to Melbourne and Adelaide. In one week in December 1851, 17,000 ounces (¾ of a ton) of gold left Forest Creek.

Commissioners continued gathering the licence fees with much enthusiasm. These men and their many assistants, dressed in smart uniforms bedecked with gold braid and medals, were nothing more than glorified tax collectors. Thirty shillings a month was a rip off, at a time when the daily wage for a tradesman was about five shillings. It represented the value of almost an ounce of gold – two hundred dollars a month in modern day value. Imagine if you had to pay two hundred dollars a month for a permit to go to work!

Perhaps it was not so much the unfair licence fee as the methods of collecting it that so angered the miners. There was the matter of 'taxation without representation', the American slogan now taken up by these new Australians. In addition, they were denied access to land, most of which was held under lease by the well-off squatters. The diggers had no representation in what passed for government but was in fact a rubber stamp for the governor and the squatters.

The Gold Commissioners

Commissioner David Armstrong was the most hated and feared of all the gold commissioners, some of whom were nothing more than gold-braided bullies. This man first appeared at Clunes early in 1851 where he enforced the law with much zeal and efficiency. Within two weeks of his arrival at Clunes, his methods caused the first ever protest meeting that eventually led to the events at the Eureka Stockade.

Keen to line his pockets, bribes were regularly handed over by diggers and storekeepers, especially the sly-grog dealers.

Armstrong was brutal and didn't hesitate to clamp men in chains or beat them severely with the heavy brass knob on his riding whip. His activities at Ballarat and Forest Creek were despised and feared. Remember that these victims were basically honest hard workers, interested primarily in making a living free from servitude to squatters and other business people. Armstrong had their tents pulled down, cut to pieces and burnt.

> BALLARAT.
> (FROM A CORRESPONDENT.)
> Golden Point, 14th Nov. 1851.
> Mr. Armstrong, one of the Commissioners for the issuing of licenses 'to dig, search for, and remove gold," has been engaged all day, accompanied by two troopers, each with a pistol in his hand, and a black fellow, in going from tent to tent, and enforcing the people to take out a gold license, whether diggers or not, including butchers, bakers, storekeepers, and others who are not diggers and have no inclination to dig, but to carry on their own proper and legitimate business of supplying the diggers and the residents on the ground with the necessaries of life, and this with a threat that, if not complied with, the tent would be cut down.

At Ballarat there was considerable relief when Armstrong was transferred to Forest Creek. Here he resumed his reign of terror and intimidation with increased zeal. His practice of sharing half the fine money with informers caused great anger. The sly-grog dealers were a special target as they faced a whopping fine of one hundred pounds. Shared two ways, or by 'arrangement', with the dealer it was quite lucrative.

The unfortunate diggers faced a fine of five pounds if found without a licence, and many preferred a cash transaction of half that directly to Armstrong. If it got to court, the penalty for having no licence was severe, usually several months of hard labour on roads and other public works. A cash payment was usually preferable.

Armstrong was eventually transferred to Wedderburn where he was finally caught up with and sacked. He openly boasted that he left the job with fifteen thousand pounds, the proceeds of his bribery and coercion.

After his death in 1883, a letter appeared in the *Bendigo Advertiser*.[4]

> Sir,—Reading in the Argus of Thursday last of the death of David Armstrong, who in the early days held the post of Inspector of Police on Bendigo, recalls to my mind an

---

4   *Bendigo Advertiser*, 4th April, 1883.

episode of those rough times in which Armstrong played a prominent part. One afternoon in December of that year a great commotion, with cries of " murder," proceeded from a grog tent belonging to a man known as Crib Williams, when I, along with the crowd, ran to see what was up. On getting there we saw Williams streaming with blood, Armstrong having gone to Williams' tent and ordered it to be pulled down. On Williams remonstrating with him, Armstrong struck him on the head with a loaded whip, which nearly killed him. The crowd were indignant, and would have lynched Armstrong on the spot, but just in the nick of time about a dozen mounted troopers arrived and surrounded Armstrong, and amidst the groaning and yelling of the crowd all rode away to the camp, some four miles distant. Now that his digger hunting days are over, it is to be hoped that he has gone to a happier hunting ground, but no one armed in a little brief authority ever acted the bully with greater gusto than David Armstrong. And many a better man than he has gone down into the grave without one word of eulogy in their favor being written by the public Press, for it was he and the like of him that exasperated the residents of the goldfields to such an extent that ultimately ended in the Eureka Stockade, where the present Speaker in the Assembly [Peter Lalor] lost an arm …

Not all Commissioners were bad or despised. For example, Assistant Commissioner Heron of the Fryerstown goldfield, was a fair and well respected person. When his tent was robbed of one thousand pounds worth of gold that he was holding in stock awaiting the gold escort to Melbourne, he was held fully responsible by the recently appointed Lieutenant-Governor Charles Hotham. Heron was ordered to repay the amount in full, the amount to be deducted from his one hundred pounds a year salary. The diggers were outraged and passed the hat around, collecting enough to pay the full amount. This demonstrates true respect. Not only that, on 4th April 1855, the diggers named a large nugget after him as a token of their respect for him.

Two new chums, on only their second day on the goldfield, sank their first hole, reopening a previously abandoned shaft in Golden Gully at

THE NEW WARDENS.

The new Wardens and their respective districts have been appointed for Castlemaine as follows—

Captain Bull, Resident Warden at Castlemaine.

Lieut. Smith, R.N., for Mount Franklyn, Yandoit, the higher branches of the Loddon, the Campaspie, and the Coliban, and all the country extending from Yandoit to the north side of the great dividing range. (This is a tract of country about 25 miles by 15. throughout which the Warden will have to decide cases of encroachment, and settle mining disputes generally !)

Mr. Heron for Fryer's Creek, Golden Point as far as Wattle Flat, south side of Forest Creek, Taradale, Back Creek, and the diggings east of the great dividing range between Golden Gully and Pennyweight Flat.

Mr. Doveton for Castlemaine, Barker's and Campbell's Creek, Forest Creek as far as Wattle Flat, Muckleford, and Tarrangower.

Fryerstown. They promptly uncovered a massive gold nugget weighing 1,023 ounces! At that time it was the largest ever found in the country. Out of respect for the Assistant Commissioner, the diggers gave him a form of immortality as they named it the Heron Nugget. The two men, Davis and Harris, put it on display before hurrying off to Port Phillip and boarding a ship home to England, where they sold it for four thousand pounds and undoubtedly enjoyed a comfortable retirement.

***

At Forest Creek, much like all the other gold centres, almost everyone owned a gun, a bit like America's wild west. Men packed guns every day, not six-guns swinging at the hip, but muzzle-loading rifles and shotguns.

In order to keep a gun clean and its mechanism working, it was the practice to fire the weapon daily. Each evening, around sundown, the gullies reverberated with the sound of hundreds of guns discharging skywards. What a sight and sound it must have been! Imagine it, in the blackness of night, hundreds of campfires, the flashes of many guns discharging and the sound of fiddlers playing their instruments somewhere.

The men of the goldfields were, in general, law-abiding people. Their guns were needed only to protect themselves, their family and their possessions. There was no other law on the goldfields, at least not for some time. Remember that almost all the police in Melbourne had deserted their posts to go looking for gold. There were few gold-seekers who ever broke the unwritten law of not working their claims on Sunday. That day was respected.

But serious unrest was growing and, no doubt, many men contemplated another use for their guns. The flames of revolution were burning brighter with every passing day.

The Rebels of Bendigo Creek

Although the Monster Meeting at Chewton justifiably lays claim to have set in train the series of meetings that led to Eureka, the story of the Red Ribbon Rebellion in Bendigo is also important. The diggings at Bendigo Creek were not immune from the developing unrest felt on other goldfields in 1851.

The settlement at Bendigo got its unusual name from a shepherd working on Gibson's run at Ravenswood. He modelled himself on the champion British boxer William Abednego 'Bendigo' Thompson. Everyone knew the shepherd as Bendigo, so the creek became Bendigo's Creek.[5]

Other people from Gibson's run also played a role in the Bendigo Creek gold strike. Mrs Kennedy, wife of the station superintendent, accompanied by her friend Mrs Farrell, wife of the station cooper, found large quantities of gold in the creek that trickled through the property. They washed a reported average of twelve ounces a day from the creek. At the same time, a Mr Henry Frencham did the same, five or six miles further north in the same creek.

The rest, as they say, is history. The rush was on! Soon the entire area swarmed with thousands of hopeful prospectors. Some fabulous finds went to the first arrivals. Thomas Morrow's party found eight pounds of surface gold, another party took two ounces every day for several weeks, another group of five men took twelve pounds of large gold from the surface in five days. The surface gold was abundant, and many fortunes were made. However, this was insignificant to the gold given up in the deep reefs in the years to follow.

On 6th June 1852, the Anti-Gold License Association was formed in Bendigo and headed up what was to become known as the Red Ribbon

---

5 In 1854, the growing metropolis was renamed Sandhurst after the British Military Academy. However, in 1891 the locals voted overwhelmingly to restore the name Bendigo.

Rebellion. Perhaps the title is a bit misleading as some might view a rebellion as an armed conflict. This was certainly not the case in Bendigo, but it came close. As on all the goldfields, the diggers generally showed respect for law and order, however, it is reported that at one large meeting in August 1852, some shots were fired. At whom, if anybody, we have no idea. In the same month, three men, Captain Brown, Doctor Jones and George Thompson, conveyed a petition to the Governor. It was rejected, but Latrobe extended hope, promising to 'examine the issue'.

At large meetings in June and July 1853, the disenchanted diggers voted to show their opposition to the gold licence and began wearing a red ribbon in their hats. At the meeting of 12th July, which was orderly, it was voted to send a deputation to Lieutenant-Governor Latrobe to convey the diggers' message and to request the reduction of the license fee from thirty shillings to ten shillings. Even that smaller amount represented a hardship to many of the workers, some of whom could not eke out any sort of worthwhile income. The request was flatly denied by Latrobe.

In July 1853, a petition circulated on all the diggings. It was said to be forty feet long and claimed to contain upwards of 30,000 signatures. An estimated 7,000 signatures, from the McIvor field, disappeared when the gold escort conveying them to Melbourne was robbed on July 20th.

A number of large meetings were conducted at Bendigo over the next year, including a gathering on Hospital Hill, attended by a very large number on 21st August 1853. One source claims that 20,000 men gathered. If so, it well surpasses the Monster Meeting at Forest Creek in December 1851, but there is no reliable source for the figure.

On 27th August, the Bendigo diggers voted to pay no more than ten shillings for a monthly licence. A deputation was sent to Police Commissioner Mitchell[6] offering the ten shilling compromise. The Commissioner rejected it and promptly rode to Melbourne to inform Latrobe that 'Bendigo was in a state of revolution.' Latrobe immediately despatched the military to keep order, making a total of 300 troopers on the goldfield.

This action further aggravated those on the field, and the diggers began to wear red ribbons in earnest. Nine out of ten displayed a red ribbon on their person, their tent, or, if a trader, their place of business.

---

6 Incidentally, the Police Commissioner was the same William Henry Fancourt Mitchell, who features earlier as the owner of Barfold Station.

A further meeting of 10,000 diggers voted to offer passive resistance. As a result, only 400 licenses were bought in September, compared with 14,000 the month before.

On 30th August 1853, Latrobe announced a new law. The licence fee would be removed and replaced by an export duty and a small registration fee. The fee was set at one pound per month or eight pounds per year, but at the same time, a licence fee of a massive fifty pounds was inflicted on each and every trader, right down to the man who humbly sold home-grown cabbages. There was no joy in that for traders or diggers alike, so their anger persisted. When the new law was put before the Legislative Council, it was rejected.

Despite this, in September, the *Argus* mistakenly announced the demise of the license and the introduction of the new law. The *Argus*, probably assumed that, as always, there would be no rejection of Latrobe's requests by the MLCs. The article stated that the tax could be considered 'gone'. Thus it was widely believed, for a time at least, that the licence had been abolished, and resistance faded. However, the traps still had the power to arrest anyone without a licence, and the digger hunts continued.

> **THE GOLD LICENCE FOLLY—HALF A MILLION PER ANNUM.**
>
> THE frantic folly of the new regulations raising the license fee to dig gold to £3 per head, per man, when viewed in its proper light, becomes a matter in which all parties interested in the maintenance of good order and good government, should take some method of interfering. We know that our views on the impolicy of this increase, are universally participated in by the thinking, and even unthinking portion of the community, but this *laissez faire* principle wont cure the evil. It must be remembered that, in reality, the increase is not *one hundred* per cent, but *eight hundred per cent!*

In June 1854, Charles Hotham took over as Lieutenant-Governor from Latrobe. The man who was held responsible for so much wrong returned to England.

Hotham had a military background and was a firm believer that orders and laws must be obeyed without question. This attitude was bound to lead to trouble. One of Hotham's first acts was to visit Ballarat with his wife. They were greeted with considerable enthusiasm and great respect, and Hotham was most impressed with this display of loyalty to the Crown. The regal couple then visited Castlemaine where they received a similarly warm welcome. This reinforced Hotham's belief that all was right with the diggers, mistaking respect for and loyalty to the royal institution for support of him and the laws.

Later, when he proclaimed that twice-weekly licence inspections (the despised digger hunts) would be carried out and the fee collected 'at all costs', the seeds of revolution were sown. Strong agitation for the total abolition of the licence tax was renewed. The *Bendigo Advertiser* wrote: 'A tax collected by armed men can never be tolerated.'

There was more trouble to come before the events at Eureka.

The Monster Meeting

In December 1851, there was great disquiet on all the goldfields, particularly with the exorbitant licence fee. The disquiet turned to fierce anger when Lieutenant-Governor Latrobe unwisely announced that the fee would double to an outrageous three pounds a month from 1st January 1852.

Almost immediately, posters began to appear, nailed to trees and buildings, calling for a protest meeting. The meeting was held and was

1851 engraving of the Monster Meeting drawn by D. Tulloch, engraved by Thomas Ham.

Glenn Braybrook at the first Monster Meeting on the site he rediscovered. The picture is signed on the back by John Ellis & Marie Jones of the Chewton Domain Society congratulating Glenn on his discovery.

attended by about 3,000 diggers. They voted to call a larger meeting on December 15th at the Shepherds Hut at the junction of Forest Creek and Wattle Creek. The wattle and daub single-roomed building with a bark roof was an outstation of William Campbell's run, Strathloddon. There was a huge roll-up as diggers came from all directions, some from as far as Bendigo. Estimates of numbers range from 8,000 to 20,000, but a more realistic figure puts it somewhere in between, probably about 12,000.

Mounting a dray set on the crest of the rise, speaker after speaker condemned Lieutenant-Governor Latrobe and his unfair taxes. There was also harsh criticism of the shutting out of ordinary men from acquiring land and setting up farms. Land, it seemed, was strictly for the use of the squatters.

However, it appears that the diggers were completely unaware that two days previously, on 13th December, Latrobe had announced in the *Government Gazette* that the increase in the license fee had been abandoned. Even in those times it was common for news to be conveyed on horseback from Melbourne to the various goldfields within 24 hours. In this instance it didn't happen. The reason such important intelligence didn't get to Forest Creek remains a subject of debate.

So, it can be argued that it was not the fear generated by the Monster Meeting that caused Latrobe's change of heart, but that it was the fear of the proposed meeting's repercussions, even to seizing of the government, if he continued with the hated licence increase. There was also the worry of serious unrest at Geelong, where armed revolt was threatened.

In any event, the increase was abandoned and the meeting is forever credited with forcing the change. In reality, even if held after the proclamation, it did – the fact that such a meeting was called was sufficient to convince the governor of his folly.

For many years, the Chewton locals were confounded by the lack of knowledge of the actual site of the meeting. Back in 1994, Doug Ralph, well known conservationist and historian, revived the idea of re-enacting the Monster Meeting as part of his protest over the amalgamation of several district shires into what is now the Shire of Mount Alexander. Doug held his small gathering in Castlemaine and, some time later, he expressed his frustration at the lack of knowledge of the actual meeting site to my son Glenn. Doug felt it was necessary to locate the actual site in order to give the gatherings authenticity and true meaning. This inspired Glenn to set about locating the site and solving the puzzle that for years had eluded the townsfolk.

Sculpture by Geoff Hocking originally placed at the site of the Monster Meeting at Forest Creek but removed by Parks officers.

> A meeting is called for 10 o'clock to morrow morning, at Agitation Hill, on the subject of the reduction of the licence-fee. The delegates from the Bendigo have arrived here, on their way to Melbourne, to take up the signatures awaiting them; and it is their intention to hold the meeting to-morrow at Castlemaine. I have just caught a sight of the petition. The signatures and petition are pasted on a strip of calico forty feet long, and has just filled it. The number of signatures amount to about ten thousand already.

The Courier *(Hobart), 2 Aug 1853, p 2.*

There had long been disagreement and even argument among the locals concerning the location of the meeting. Some claimed it was behind the Mount Alexander Hotel, others said it was on Post Office Hill. The 1995 re-enactment leaflet actually placed it on Post Office Hill, while at the same time, the Tourist Information Board put it at the intersection of the Pyrenees Highway and Golden Point Road. All this was conjecture, but the last guess was getting warmer. There was still some way to go.

'HISTORIC SITE IDENTIFIED' was the exciting headline in the *Castlemaine Mail* on 4th June 2004. The article reported:

> 'The site of the fabled great Meeting of Miners at Forest Creek in December 1851 has been pinpointed at Chewton. The discovery has excited many people, including Professor Weston Bate, former lecturer in History at Melbourne University and President of the Royal Historical Society of Victoria.'

An old map that had been bequeathed to the Domain Society by the late Barbara James was held in the Chewton Town Hall. The map was the work of Surveyor WS Urquhart in 1853. One day Glenn was examining it and he noticed that it showed a shepherd's hut as one of the survey reference points. Armed with that and a copy of David Tulloch's now famous drawing of the meeting, as well as a sketch by an unknown artist, he went looking for the location. 'It didn't take me long to find the likely spot. The map appeared to show the hut near the side of Golden Point Road.'

So, in January 2002, Glenn reported in the *Chewton Chat* that he was confident that he had found the hut's location. 'Using the map and drawings, I believe it possible that I can identify the exact spot.'

No further action was generated immediately, but Glenn was determined to prove his find. He next engaged my help and I was able to convert the old imperial measurements to metric and hold one end of his lengthy measuring tape. Comparing the result of that thorough exercise with the landscape and map details used before, Glenn was finally satisfied. Of particular value was the sketch by the unknown artist which clearly showed the background hills to the north-west.

Glenn told the *Mail*: 'It was a pretty exciting time as we stood where, beneath our feet, was the long-lost hut site, and therefore the Monster

Meeting site. We placed a stray piece of granite pitcher on the spot and went home.'

The *Mail* continued: 'Glenn took his theory, the map and drawings to David Bannear, Archaeological Adviser to Heritage Victoria, who consulted with Clive Willman from Geological Survey. They overlaid the old map with one of today and were able to pinpoint the exact position of the original hut.' They decided it was precisely where Glenn had said it was! A later newspaper article featured a beaming Glenn on the site of the shepherd's hut that he had positively identified. It was a proud time for him.

Now there was considerable interest and excitement! Professor Weston Bate told the *Mail* and my audience on local radio that the importance of the newly rediscovered site could not be overestimated. The Ballarat Reform League took up the cause and arranged and funded proper recognition.

The spot is now marked with a stone cairn and descriptive brass signage and is the basis for the annual re-enactment of the original 1851 Monster Meeting on the edge of Forest Creek. It is held on what is positively the site of Shepherds Hut.

I am proud that my son is the one who identified the site. The late Doug Ralph would be smiling.

Another large meeting in Castlemaine.

In May 1853 about 1,000 people from all walks of life met on Agitation Hill, where the Anglican Church now stands, to protest over a raid by tax collectors on a boarding house proprietor. Troopers had raided the house of a Mr McMahon and arrested him, alleging he was selling sly grog. He was not, and was promptly acquitted by the court. The locals were angered by this attack on a popular, law-abiding citizen. There were angry speeches and the meeting resolved to 'resist the despotic invasion of people's constitutional rights.'

There were many such smaller meeting across the goldfields, but Forest Creek stands apart because it was the largest ever. But there is still the claim of 20,000 gathered at Hospital Hill in Bendigo. Was that gathering bigger than the Monster Meeting at Forest Creek two years before?

The Eureka Stockade

Diggers first showed their combined opposition to the thirty shillings (one pound ten shillings) a month licence fee at Buninyong in September 1851. It was the first of many meetings over the next three years. The surprising thing is that the diggers accepted the tax and the methods used to collect it for so long.

The digger hunts became a sport for the goldfield commissioners and their assistants. The diggers also considered it something of a sport. As the commissioners approached, the cry of 'Joe' went up, and men would scurry in every direction, down shafts and into tunnels, even if they held a licence. The troopers were the servants of Lieutenant-Governor Charles Joseph Latrobe, variously known to the diggers as Charlie Joe or Governor Joey.[7] This is undoubtedly where 'Joe' originated.

When Latrobe announced that his tax would increase to three pounds a month from 1st January 1852 there was uproar. More meetings of outraged diggers followed this announcement, including the Monster Meeting at Forest Creek on December 15th 1851. Sensing at last that there was real danger of an uprising, Latrobe rescinded his decision in a notice published on December 13th, too late it seems for word to get to Forest Creek in time to cancel the planned meeting.

Late in 1854, at Ballarat, the licence inspections were increased to twice weekly, which aggravated the already dangerous mood of the diggers. Organised resistance was called for and the Ballarat Reform League was formed.

* * *

On 7th October 1854, digger James Scobie was murdered outside Bentley's Eureka Hotel. James Bentley was charged with Scobie's murder but was acquitted. This enraged the diggers who were sure that Bentley had committed the murder. They were convinced that Magistrate John Dewes had been paid off by Bentley to find him innocent.

A protest meeting was called outside the pub. Up to 3,000 diggers passed resolutions to be presented to the Lieutenant-Governor expressing their disapproval of the way in which the court decision had been reached.

---

7   *The Argus*, Sat 10 Jun 1899, p. 4.

As the meeting dispersed, the troopers followed some diggers, others stopped their homeward trek to see what was going on, or what was going to happen. There was general movement towards Bentley's hotel. At first gravel was thrown, then more damage was done, until all the windows were broken. Some of the diggers got inside and started destroying the furniture and fittings. Bentley, meanwhile, had made his escape on horseback out the back.

When everything had been destroyed, someone, very deliberately, in front of the troopers, set a fire on the windward side of the bowling alley at the back of the hotel. The animals were released and the stables were set alight. Anything of Bentley's was added to the fire, even his wife's jewellery box. The musicians' instruments were saved, and the staff's possessions were put in a safe place. The crowd had grown to eight or ten thousand.

A dray was pushed into the fire, but when somebody said it wasn't Bentley's, it was pulled out again. Then somebody else said that it was Bentley's, so it was pushed back in. Water barrels were broken so that the fire could not be extinguished. As was a barrel of porter (heavy beer).

The final act was to rummage through the ashes for any surviving bottles of spirit or ale and start the revelry. One man was arrested, but was 'detached' from the troopers on their way to the Camp.

A petition was sent to the lieutenant-governor restating the evidentiary details of the three prosecution witnesses and the three witnesses for the defence. They stated that the obvious ruling in law should have been to refer the case to trial by jury, not the total exoneration of the defendant.

> 'Your petitioners are borne out in this view of the case by the authority of Lord Denman, (Magistrates' Manual, page 21) who states, "if witnesses for the defence contradict those for the prosecution in material points, then the case would be properly sent to a jury to ascertain the truth of the statements of each party." Your petitioners beg to state, that not only the decision, but also the manner in which the case was conducted, both by the magistrates, and the coroner, has strongly tended to destroy the confidence hitherto placed in them by the public.
>
> 'Trusting that your Excellency will be pleased to attribute the object of your petitioners to its real motive, namely a love

of order and justice, and that your Excellency will graciously grant their request.'

Eventually, the Lieutenant Governor ordered a new trial of Bentley along with the co-accused – his wife and two men named John Farrell and Hervey Hance. The trial took place on Saturday 18th November, 1854.

> The jury retired at a quarter to nine to consider their verdict, and returned into court at twenty five minutes to ten, when their foreman gave in their verdict, as follows:- James Francis Bentley, guilty of manslaughter; Catherine Bentley, not guilty; John Farrell, guilty of manslaughter; Hervey Hance, guilty of manslaughter.

The guilty men were each sentenced to three years imprisonment with hard labour on the roads or other public works.

However, anger remained, and there was serious talk of a Republic. At Government House there was fear that the diggers would attempt to overthrow the government.

In November 1854, Lieutenant-Governor Hotham ordered more troops to Ballarat. They were greeted by the diggers with abuse (needled with cries of 'Joey, Joey') and the throwing of stones and debris. Some of their carts were overturned.

The following day, thousands of men rallied on Bakery Hill, and the digger's flag, the beautiful, simply designed Southern Cross, was hoisted for the first time. The meeting elected Peter Lalor as the digger's leader, and many men burnt their licences in a gesture of defiance.

The next day, with unbelievable recklessness considering the mood of the men, Commissioner Rede ordered a great licence hunt. It was strongly resisted and men pelted the tax collectors with stones and abuse.

Sir Charles Hotham 1806–1855

The men gathered on Eureka Lead and erected a makeshift stockade –

it was more of a training ground than a headquarters to be defended.

Saturday night, 2nd December 1854, most of the men had departed the stockade, in the knowledge that, the next day being Sunday and strictly observed, there would be no action. Only about 120 diggers remained in the stockade. Commissioner Rede had other ideas and was busy planning for the next morning. 'We must crush this democratic agitation', he said. 'We must catch them with arms in their hands.'

Before dawn on a Sunday morning that will remain forever infamous, Rede ordered 276 soldiers and police to attack the stockade. Totally unprepared, the diggers were quickly overcome.

There followed an orgy of killing by the soldiers. Even the wounded lying helpless on the ground were bayoneted. The military burnt the stockade and the tents with their meagre contents. It was senseless cruelty and unforgivable brutality. The sun rose on twenty-six dead diggers and six dead soldiers.

Many wounded diggers, including the badly injured Peter Lalor, were spirited away. We will never know how many of them later died from their wounds.

Thirteen diggers were arrested and charged with treason. At their trial they were all acquitted.[8]

> Yesterday all was quiet up to 11 o'clock, and would have been so yet had not the attempt been made to look for licenses; some of those who were first asked, instead of licenses I believe showed their cards of membership of the Reform League, and when about to be taken into custody escaped among the Gravel Pits workings; more force was soon sent for and arrived, they drew up on the New Road, when Messrs. Rede & Johnstone advanced in front of them to a crowd, the former gentleman tried to persuade those assembled and still gathering to disperse, failing to do this he said he must read the Riot Act. and use force; several parties remonstrated with him, on the impolicy of the course he was following. Mr Rede replied that he was merely carrying out the law as it at present stood, and that he was determined to do do at all hazards. He then began to read the Riot Act, at which time I was standing near him, as a large body of troops and foot police, were at some distance behind me, I considered it my safer course to shift my quarters, which I did, but soon found that the Riot Act had been got through at such a telegraphic speed. that notwithstanding a thrice repeated, God save the diggers, I was well nigh caught in the rush of troopers, consequent on the order "draw swords and advance."

---

8   Amusingly, the judge at the trial, William A'Beckett, sentenced two members of the gallery to a week in prison for contempt of court, shown by their rowdy applause when the jury declared its verdict.

In 1855, as a result of the disaster and the subsequent community anger and unrest, the obnoxious licence was replaced by a Miners Right costing one pound per month or eight pounds a year. Soon, elected warders replaced the appointed administrators and the Legislative Council was enlarged, and five members were to hold a Miners Right.

Peter Lalor and John Basson Humffray, both heroes of Eureka, were elected to represent the goldfields – a major step toward manhood suffrage. All this was passed into law in 1857. Eureka, with its government-ordered slaughter of good men, is the basis of our democracy, it was this event that forced the changes.

John Foster, Governor Hotham's Colonial Secretary, stated: 'An attempt to vindicate the law and to increase revenue lost both the law and the revenue.'

Although they lost on the battlefield, the diggers of Ballarat won a great victory for the people.

Should this be our national flag? It has far more meaning to Australia than the British Blue Ensign which is the basis of our present national symbol. It was the events of Eureka, under the hand-sewn Southern Cross, that forced the democratic changes on an authoritarian government. It is a flag we can stand beneath with real pride.

Raffaello Carboni

Italian-born Raffaello Carboni is famed as the writer of the only eyewitness account of the 1854 massacre of diggers at Eureka, in his book *The Eureka Stockade*, published by him in 1855.[9]

It is little known that he also had knowledge of the members of the Dja Dja Wurrung people. In 1853 he left the goldfields and took a job as a shepherd at a property in the Loddon valley. Unfortunately he did not record its exact whereabouts, but there is very strong indication that it was close to the Loddon River.

He mentions his experience briefly in chapter five of his book: he 'got among the blacks, the whole Tarrang tribe in corobory.' This meant that he actually lived with the Dja Dja Wurrung people for a short period, in which time he studied their customs, and particularly their language. He said he 'soon picked up bits of their yabber yabber'. Of the women he was not complimentary; 'their Lubras ugly enough; not so however the slender arms and small hands of their young girls, though the fingers were rather long.'

He embarked on preparing notes for an Italian-Aboriginal dictionary, but apparently it was never completed. He spoke highly of the fine landscape of this run on the Loddon and in glowing terms of the quality of the Loddon water: 'Tea out of this Loddon magnificent.' After a short time, 'got the gold fever again and I started for old Ballaarat.'

What a pity he didn't stay longer and write much more of his time with the local people.

He described the events at Eureka, including:

> ... the redcoats rushed with fixed bayonets to storm the stockade. ... the job was done too quickly for their wonted ardour, for they actually thrust their bayonets on the body of the dead and wounded strewed about on the ground.
>
> The troopers, enjoying the fun within the stockade, now spread it without. The tent next to mine (Quinn's) was soon in a blaze. I collected in haste my most important papers, and

---

9   Available for download from the Gutenberg Project (gutenberg.org/ebooks/3546).

Thirteen diggers, including Raphelo (Carboni) were tried on the capital charge of treason. They were all acquitted. Mount Alexander Mail *2nd March 1855.*

rushed out to remonstrate against such a wanton cruelty. Sub-inspector Carter pointing with his pistol ordered me to fall in with a batch of prisoners. There were no two ways: I obeyed. In the middle of the gully, I expostulated with Captain Thomas, he asked me whether I had been made a prisoner within the stockade. "No, sir," was my answer. He noticed my frankness, my anxiety and grief. After a few words more in explanation, he, giving me a gentle stroke with his sword, told me "If you really are an honest digger, I do not want you, sir; you may return to your tent."

Carboni returned to the stockade shortly after to help tend to the wounded, some of whom were moved to the London Hotel, which is where he was arrested at gun point some hours later. He was among the thirteen tried and acquitted of treason.

The Forgotten Meeting

On the subject of diggers' meetings, the following is the local newspaper account of Castlemaine's largest meeting. It is known as the Forgotten Meeting.

Much is heard of the Bendigo Red Ribbon Rebellion and the Monster Meeting at Forest Creek, but little of what the *Mount Alexander Mail*

Extraordinary of 11th December 1854, edition 32,[10] described as 'The greatest meeting ever held in Castlemaine.'

It's uncertain how many attended, but the newspaper estimated 4,000. Nor is it known for certain where it was held, as the *Mail* article does not mention that, but it was obviously a major event in the fledgling township. One claim is twenty thousand diggers, but a more likely figure is the newspaper's four thousand. Some say it was in Market Square, others suggest the hill to the west, known as Agitation Hill, but nobody is sure. It was, however, the largest assembly of persons in Castlemaine, remembering that the Monster Meeting was at neighbouring Forest Creek.

The Saturday meeting, which had been called to hear the report of the delegation to Lieutenant-Governor Hotham concerning the grievances of diggers, took on new meaning with the news of the 'disturbance' in Ballarat the previous Sunday. News of the slaughter of the diggers at Eureka was circulated quickly to all the goldfields and there was much anger in the air.

The meeting was addressed in turn by members of the delegation, principally locals Doctor Hambrook and Mr Palmer, with Captain Trewartha and Mr Denovan from the Reform League. The meeting set out to embrace the principles of both the Ballarat and Bendigo Reform Leagues, already united.

Commissioner Bull and a handful of other officials attended, maintaining a low profile. They were politely received.

Captain Trewartha opened proceedings, and Dr Hambrook was elected chairman. He outlined the result of the delegation's discussions with Lieutenant-Governor Hotham, an apparently trustworthy and honourable man. The Governor had assured them that he had appointed a Commission to attend the goldfields and report back on the various grievances of the diggers. Principal among these were the Gold Licence tax, the non-representation of ordinary people in the government, and the denial of land for settlement by non-squatters. Dr Hambrook stated that any other business would be heard at the end of the meeting. This

---

10 The *Mount Alexander Mail Extraordinary* was the masthead of this unusual issue of the paper. It was of two pages, devoted entirely to the meeting, probably the only edition ever to bear the title. The report of the meeting was repeated in the normal issue of the paper on the following Friday.

was greeted with resounding angry cries of 'Ballarat. Ballarat', as men were impatient for this to be addressed.

Dr. Hambrook went on to thank John Pascoe Fawkner for his support of the diggers in obtaining the audience with the Governor.

'The diggers are entirely unrepresented in government,' he said. 'Government members seem to think that their college education alone is sufficient for them to legislate for the rest of us.' Loud hissing and boos came from the audience. More cries of 'Ballarat' filled the air.

He continued: 'The 660 people of the gentlemen class have 18 representatives in government. We diggers have none.' More shouts and hisses greeted this announcement. 'Let every digger have a voice.' Cries again of 'Ballarat!'

He went on: 'The weight of moral force is with us. Let there be no violence or use of weapons.' This drew many angry shouts with calls like, 'What did that do for Ballarat?'

Delegate Mr. Palmer reiterated the statements of the other speakers. 'Governor Hotham deserves a chance. He differs from the arrogance of Latrobe.' He concurred with the widely held contempt for the previous governor.

The diggers then voted to accept that Lieutenant-Governor Hotham would attend to their grievances and went on to elect a local committee to adopt the principles of the Ballarat and Bendigo Reform Leagues.

Next came the discussion that the men most wanted to hear – Eureka.

Speaker after speaker expressed their anger over the events at Ballarat. Mr Denovan spoke of the injustice and humiliation constantly inflicted on diggers. He talked of the meeting where licences were burned and of Commissioner Robert William Rede's reckless act of following this with digger hunts with a vengeance. He repudiated claims that the strife was caused by foreigners – Americans, Frenchmen and Germans. 'They were Australians. They knew no distinction of country. They were not responsible, it was the government.'

A passionate Mr Denovan said: 'It was the government that desecrated the Sabbath by the slaughter of good Christian men.' This brought on many curses and cries from the diggers and one called loudly, 'It won't happen here.' The men were angry and words like foul, unworthy, illegal and barbaric flourished.

Mr Denovan continued, 'Shame on the government. These men were not rioters, they were simple diggers who met to remedy their grievances.

This is the last resort of weeping democracy.'

He described the scene at Eureka:

> 'Unclaimed dead remained on the ground and when the police fired the stockade the flesh was roasted from their bones. Their names deserve to be preserved for posterity as the heroes of Australia.'

There was great cheering, and Mr Donovan asked each man to wear a black band of crepe on their hats and a red ribbon to express their esteem for the memory of the dead men of Eureka. The hat on every head was lifted in quiet observance as the meeting was closed.

Castlemaine quickly sold out of black crepe and red ribbon, so men tore red shirts and cloths into strips to display on tents and to wear on coats and hats.

The spirit of the men who died at Eureka filled every heart at Castlemaine that day.

> Business was entirely suspended on Saturday, and our auction postponed on account of the "monster" meeting at View Point. "Red ribbon," after the meeting on Saturday, rose from 6d. to 17d. per yard, and eagerly purchased.
> JONES & CO., Auctioneers.

The Celestials abound

The Celestial Empire was a very old name used to refer to China, and so the term 'Celestials' was often used to describe the Chinese immigrants on the goldfields (not just in Australia, but also in Canada and the United States).

The Chinese were an important part of the population of this land in the days of gold. In fact, they made up to a quarter of the population on some goldfields.

From 1852, Chinese men began to arrive on the goldfields of Ballarat and thence to Mount Alexander and on to Dai Gum San, the Big Gold Mountain – Bendigo. They brought with them a distinctive way of life and special skills in finding gold. More than that, many began to play an important role in providing food from their extensive market gardens for the diggers. All they needed was a patch of ground, some water and any kind of manure, human or otherwise! Their produce was important in providing nutrition and helped prevent illness and death. Some remnants of the gardens can be seen at Vaughn and Glenluce. These garden remnants are now part of the Castlemaine Diggings National Heritage Park. One legacy is the wild spring onions that appear along the banks of the Loddon River from time to time. In Castlemaine, there were several Chinese market gardens, located approximately opposite what is now the South Primary School and the old gasworks site.

One of the last of about fifteen Joss Houses stood nearby in Greenhill Avenue, below Ten Foot Hill. Sadly it was demolished over a century ago.

It is probable that two thousand Chinese lived in Castlemaine. Near the South Primary School of today they established a village consisting mainly of calico tents. It was complete, with a Joss House, opium dens (opium was legal), gambling tents, herbalists and much more. It was a thriving township. However, the population was almost entirely male, with perhaps only two or three women. The Celestials lived quietly, except on those occasions when they celebrated festivals with the beating

Chinese leave Flemington for the Mount Alexander goldfields. Watercolour Samuel Brees. SLV.

of drums and the explosions of thousands of firecrackers as they formed processions through the streets. This annoyed some people, but most enjoyed the spectacle.

A very large problem with the village was poor drainage and the lack of hygienic amenities. Most of the waste was deposited straight into Forest Creek. Eventually, the village was moved to what is now the Western Reserve. Here a similar tent town was rebuilt, but drainage was considerably improved.

There was certainly bigotry and racism directed at the Chinese. There were also false allegations made against them. Their habit of smoking opium didn't go over very well with many Europeans, who failed to understand that this practice was as normal to them as the diggers downing a few beers at their favourite pub.

Their fraternising with the local 'girls' wasn't viewed very kindly either. (Remember that there were precious few women amongst all these men).

Decorations salvaged from the Castlemaine Joss house. Courtesy George Milford.

The last Chinese Joss House in Castlemaine. Picture courtesy Museum of Victoria. Held by Castlemaine Pioneers and Old Residents Association.

Chinese on stagecoach, probably at Newstead c1853 bound for Fiddlers Creek. Courtesy of Eureka Centre Ballarat.

Apparently there was a lane off Forest Street that held places of ill-repute. A contemporary writer said, in part:

> '- never be believed that our Saxon and Norman girls could sink as low as to consort with such a herd of Gorilla Devils. Devilish and leprous in feature and devilish in nature also.'

Along the flats beside Campbell's Creek and Guildford, other Chinese villages sprang up, all similarly equipped. No trace of these remains, as every remnant has been swept away by numerous floods. Indeed, considering the extent of Chinese presence on the goldfields, very little evidence remains to indicate that the Chinese were ever there in large numbers. For example, in Castlemaine and Guildford, the only indications are some headstones and ceremonial ovens in cemeteries.

By 1858, such was the resentment of the huge influx of Chinese, with the population now measuring one in ten, that the Victorian Government introduced a ten pounds landing tax on every new Celestial arrival[11]. This

---

11   The Act was officially titled: An Act to Make Provision for Certain Immigrants. In the preamble it was stated that '... the word "Immigrant" shall mean any male adult native of China or its dependencies or of any islands in the Chinese Seas or any person born of Chinese parents.'

was a huge sum at that time – compare it to the one pound ten shilling gold licence fee that many found impossible to pay. A way around it was promptly found: The ships unloaded their human cargo at Robe in South Australia and the men undertook a five hundred kilometre walk to the goldfields. Today we are reminded of these walkers by 'Chinaman's Wells'. Along the route, they dug wells to provide water to supply those who followed. Between 1857 and 1863 some 17,000 men made the exhausting walk. Deprived of proper food, and enduring the most difficult circumstances, the mortality rate was high.

Some good came of it, however. In 1854, a gold discovery was made near the walkers' route at Pinky Point near Ararat. There was a rush, and it became known as the Mount William goldfield. Then, in 1857, a group of Chinese walkers uncovered much gold at what became the Canton Lead. Of course, many of the Chinese stayed on to work the land there. Ararat became one of the major goldfields.

While most of the Chinese on the goldfield had come from their homeland, a small number had sailed from the goldfields of California, one of whom was Lee Heng Jakjung. He settled at Fryers Creek and became a well-respected citizen. Having a strong command of English, he was often used as an interpreter by the Gold Commissioners and occasionally by the courts. He married a local girl and lived out his life a respected member of the community.

Things were not always as good for his fellow countrymen, as there was considerable dislike, fear and resentment toward them from Europeans. This was probably brought on by a misunderstanding of them and their different ways. There was also a feeling that they were taking gold that was really the property of the Europeans. The fact that they worked together in solid groups and generally kept to themselves in their own communities did not help either. There was a reason behind their methodology. By working together they were better able to locate gold, and their numbers acted as protection from attacks and abuse by other diggers, which was a common occurrence.

Often they were referred to as 'sojourners', a derogatory term indicating the belief that they were here with the sole purpose of gaining money, with no intention of settling. They would return to their home country as soon as they had gathered sufficient wealth. This was largely correct. Only fifteen per cent of the European diggers ever returned home, but about sixty per cent of the Chinese did so, as soon as they had repaid any indentures and could show sufficient wealth left over to make a triumphant return to their families. The reason so few Europeans went home, especially the low-caste British, was that they probably had very little worth returning to, other than family.

The Chinese gold diggers worked hard, but, like most diggers, the majority remained desperately poor. It was rare indeed for a man to take more than a hundred pounds home with him to China.

To many Europeans, the Celestials were alien – even hated by some. Vilification was common and there many race-based incidents, but few, if any, resulted in deaths. In the biggest race-based riots, at Lambing Flat (now Young) in NSW and Buckland River in Victoria, there were no fatalities. There were, however, a number of serious injuries and major destruction of property of the Chinese diggers.

In Castlemaine in 1860, a group of Christian people decided to build a Chinese chapel in Mostyn Street. Its purpose was to hopefully save the 'heathen Celestials'. Enough money was quickly raised from public subscription, including two hundred pounds from the Methodist Church,

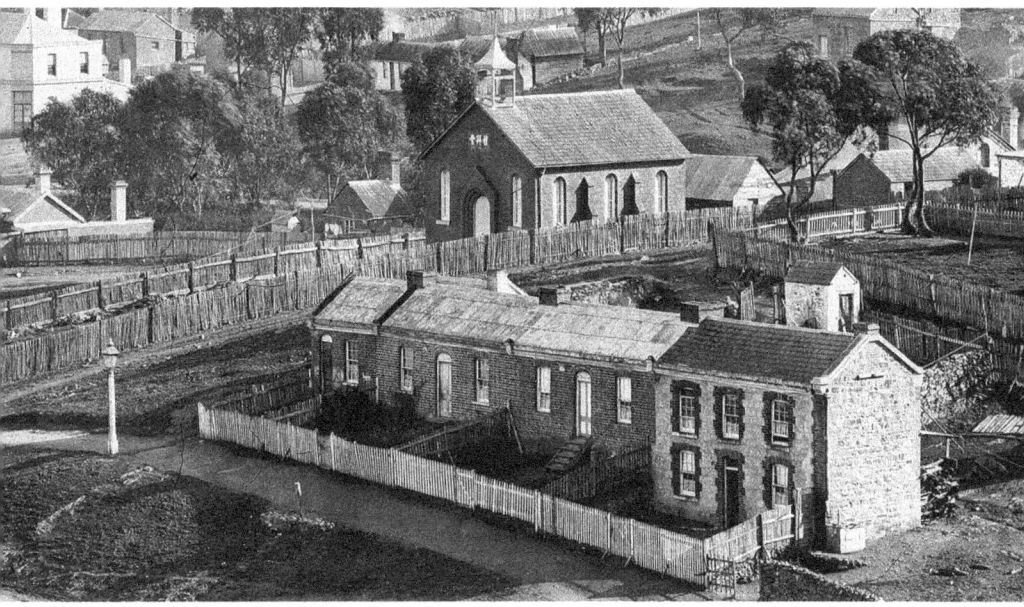

The Chinese Chapel in Mostyn Street Castlemaine, built in 1860, is at the rear of the picture. It no longer exsists. Picture courtesy State Library of NSW and Chris Long.

for the work to begin. A modest brick building resulted. At the laying of the foundation stone, the principal speaker, Reverend Mr Blamiers, said the chapel would give the 'opportunity to sow good seeds in their heathen minds.' The chapel was small, 25 feet by 18 feet, but sufficient for the purpose, as only a few Celestials attended regular services. However, there was some success, with a small number of men being converted.

***

There was a steady decline in the numbers of Chinese remaining in Australia, and by 1863 the rush to the new discoveries in New Zealand probably spelled the end of any further Chinese arrivals. Their population numbers stabilised by the end of the century. Today 1.2 million Australians have Chinese ancestry.

Comparatively few people of Chinese descent remain in most goldfields areas today. One exception is Bendigo where an estimated 1,500 citizens are descended from Chinese diggers. They form a very important and active part of the community and contribute considerably to the community. The famous Sun Loong dragon and the hugely popular Easter Fair are good examples of the influence of Chinese culture on the life of the city. Under the leadership of the inspirational Russell Jack, the community has established the Bendigo Chinese Museum. Among its many exhibits are several beautiful ceremonial dragons which are the focus of the Easter Fair.

Part Four

The Railway

The Iron Road Cometh

The advent of the Murray River Railway had a far-reaching effect on central and northern Victoria. It was to prove to be the life-blood for a number of towns – Castlemaine is a notable example. The *Argus* of 4th July 1855 reported that there was much discussion and excitement regarding a route under consideration for a railway connecting Melbourne to Williamstown, and another to Geelong and then on to Ballarat. The planned Murray River route would run from Ballarat, through the Loddon Valley, to an as yet unidentified centre on the mighty river. Sandhurst and Castlemaine did not appear to be on that route. There were consequent rumblings. More discussions would follow, not all good news, but…

To prepare for the construction of the proposed railway, a private company, the Murray River and Mount Alexander Railway Company, had been established in 1853 under the presidency of early settler and 'disgustingly rich' squatter Charles Ebden. The company's objective was to bring to reality the railways that had been under so much discussion. A generous and supportive government kicked the company along with a grant of fifty acres of land at Batman's Hill for the required railway terminus (today, the hill no longer exists, it is the site of the Southern Cross station, previously Spencer Street station).

Sadly, the company encountered financial difficulty and went to the wall in 1856, lasting fewer than three years. It had achieved very little, except some earthworks on the Williamstown line and basic preparatory work on the Geelong project.

All was not lost, however, as the government boldly stepped in. Governor Hotham advised the Legislative Council of his belief that the government could undertake the construction of railways by borrowing from the London market.

Top: Batmans Hill as it was in 1840.
Centre: Removing the last of Batmans Hill.
Bottom: Site of Batmans Hill in 1892.

The councillors accepted Hotham's advice and engaged a former lieutenant in the Royal Engineers, Andrew Clarke,[1] as surveyor general, to negotiate the purchase of the bankrupt railway company and assets. After much talk and letter writing he eventually bought the company for just sixty-eight thousand pounds. The government was in the railway business and has remained so ever since. The Victorian Railways Department was created to run the railway system.

Andrew Clarke appointed talented civil engineer George Darbyshire as principal in charge of design and construction, and he began work almost immediately. It seems that governments can work efficiently when the need arises.

Andrew Clarke proved to be a good choice, and under his direction, and that of Darbyshire, marvellous feats of engineering were to take place. Both men insisted that British standards be adopted, including the 5' 3" gauge, as well as being double-track. As a result, Victoria has always had a superior rail infrastructure to NSW, for example.

Which way the railway?

In modern times, Castlemaine and the Mount Alexander Shire have established a reputation for community division, objection and argument. It was not always like that, in fact just the opposite. Once, citizens rarely got excited by decisions made by governments, councils, businesses or individuals. However, a couple of railway-related decisions, or threats of decisions, quickly got the people to their feet.

The initial Murray River plan was quite attractive to the government. They would simultaneously build the lines to Williamstown and Geelong and then to Ballarat. From that gold-laden centre, the tracks would run via the Loddon Valley to a point on the Murray River. This route presented less difficulty than any others that had been suggested.

The sticking point was having the railway go through Ballarat, and some citizens were not impressed. At Sandhurst (Bendigo) there was absolute outrage! This was an unbelievable insult. Wasn't Bendigo the richest and most progressive town in the colony? Such a route would

---

1   Andrew Clarke was the son of the Governor of Western Australia and a cousin of Marcus Clarke, author of *For the Term of His Natural Life*.

pass thirty miles to the west of their town and would bring to an end the future importance dreamed of by its business people and the general citizenry. And what of Castlemaine? The uproar from both Sandhurst and Castlemaine quickly found its way to parliament.

On 4th September 1856, the *Argus* informed its readers that a decision on the railway route as far as Gisborne had finally been settled. It ran through Footscray and Diggers Rest to Mount Aitken, curved east of Bald Hill to Sunbury and proceeded through the many rises to Gisborne. While there was much celebration in those towns, the rest of the route to Sandhurst was still under discussion.

Also in September 1856, there were several newspaper reports that rankled the locals, residents and business-people alike. For example, the *Portland Guardian* reported that the government was determined that the proposed rail to Sandhurst would bypass Castlemaine, as this option would be too costly and too difficult.

In January 1857, the *Argus* posted an article that caused concern in Castlemaine. It was being considered, if not already decided, that Castlemaine would be bypassed and that Harcourt was to be made the rail centre, with only a branch line to Castlemaine. Due to the rough terrain from the junction to Castlemaine, the cost savings would be considerable. Another possible route from the Elphinstone junction, through the Major's Pass at a cost of 1.2 million pounds was considered, but quickly discarded.

Was Castlemaine to be reduced to a mere branch line?

Castlemaine locals refused to be silent. There was loud and vigorous protest. 'Are we to hang onto the skirts of the railway project?' 'Is Castlemaine, a flourishing township, to play second fiddle to obscure Harcourt?'

On 11th September 1857, the *Ballarat Star* announced that the Parliament had listened. Twenty-seven of the thirty-eight members voted to take the line through Castlemaine via Chewton and then on to Harcourt. There was much joy in Castlemaine.

It was definite! Castlemaine business people and its 6,000 residents heaved a mighty sigh of relief. Had the town been bypassed, Castlemaine would almost certainly have withered on the vine and become, much as Maldon is today, a quiet town without industry and very few people, however peaceful it might be. Some present day Castlemaine people think maybe it would have been a good thing! The decision to include the township of Castlemaine in the mix had a lasting and hugely beneficial effect, as can be seen today.

* * *

In March 1858, tenders were called for the construction of a total of 206 miles of track. The Melbourne to Sandhurst section was awarded to Cornish and Bruce for almost three and a half million pounds.

The first obstacle for the builders was the Great Dividing Range. Where the line now crosses the Great Divide near Mount Macedon, the elevation is 570 metres. In a wonderful engineering achievement, a track rising of just 1 in 50 was achieved, in some sections it has a rise of only 1 in 90.

Beyond the Dividing Range lay some really serious obstacles. Numerous bridges were required, including the massive structures at Malmsbury and Taradale. These tasks were difficult enough, but things were made more so by the decision to route the line from Elphinstone to Castlemaine. Among other things, it required the construction of a very long tunnel, a formidable task. This job involved the huge excavation of the east and west approaches, the construction of eight culverts and blasting through hard rock. A large dam, know today as Railway Dam, was also built as part of the process.

Progress from Melbourne was rapid, and by January 1859, the line to Sunbury was opened. Tragedy struck soon after with the death of John Cornish in March, leaving William Bruce in control. However, the excellent choice of George Darbyshire as chief engineer kept the project in good hands.

George Darbyshire was generally well regarded as a good man, excellent in his job. Then, unhappily and for reasons never revealed, he was subjected to malicious, unsubstantiated and probably false attacks in the press, particularly by the *Argus*. He was ultimately forced to resign his position, which was given to Thomas Higginbotham, also a good choice, as he had considerable railway experience in England. He was appointed Engineer-in-Chief of Victorian Railways.

Shortly after the opening of the line to Sunbury and the death of Cornish, John Bruce, the other partner of the contractors Cornish and Bruce, moved to Castlemaine to be nearer the new centre of action.

The Big Hill tunnel.

Tunnels, bridges, culverts and viaducts

By the early 1860s, the Elphinstone tunnel construction had reached a point where excavation of the approaches was well underway. Several hundred men were engaged exclusively in blasting a way through solid rock. The air was filled with constant explosions from work on the two approaches. Other gangs of tradesmen and assistants were engaged in building eight substantial culverts to drain the expected rush of water from the surrounding embankments and natural rock formations. To hold the water, a huge storage dam was built. As well, there was considerable road construction as part of the project. Massive mounds of excavated rock and soil were deposited nearby and are still clearly visible, although now well covered with timber regrowth. In fact, a disused road to Fryerstown, appears to be formed on top of one of the mounds.

Such were the numbers employed that a small village sprang up just to the west of the site. It is possible that another was located to the east, but no evidence has been found. There is ample evidence of the western site. I have visited it several times with Glenn and once with the late

Doug Ralph who knew the history well. He believed that as many as three hundred lived there. Remains of walls and foundations are still visible and an archaeological dig would be worthwhile. Doug told me of the grog shanty that was there and pointed to the remains of a cellar. Broken bottles litter the area.

The author at the cellar of a grog shop at the site of the Elphinstone tunnel shanty town.

In the shanty town, booze was a real problem, fuelled by a number of sly-grog shops. Wages were eight shillings a day for unskilled men and fourteen shillings a day for masons and bricklayers. Paydays heralded brawls among the men, and it became necessary to place two police constables permanently on-site to keep things under control. There was a fifty pound fine and four months jail with hard labour for

The viaduct at Taradale

offenders. However, it appeared difficult to make an arrest, let alone gain a conviction. The *Mount Alexander Mail* lamented the fact that one Judge Forbes had ruled that any police or stooges buying grog from the purveyors of illegal booze, were equally guilty under the law and to be treated as accomplices. His ruling was later overturned on appeal.

The construction of the tunnel was a huge undertaking, even more difficult than the one at Big Hill, Bendigo, which was dug through solid granite, the reason being the comparative ease of construction at the approaches at Big Hill.

At Elphinstone, according to figures published in a Public Works Report of May 18th 1860, a massive amount of excavation was required. For the east and west approaches alone about 527,000 cubic yards of soil and rock were removed. From the tunnel, another 410,000 cubic yards – an estimated total of 937,000 cubic yards. All this with manpower and horsedrawn equipment!

The 385 metre long tunnel (the tunnel at Big Hill was longer by just five metres) was completely lined with countless thousands of bricks that appear to be supported by nothing but air; this alone was a massive task. Overall, it was a major engineering achievement for the time.

In a job this size, employing so many people, there were a number of disputes involving both workers and management. However, there were only two serious strikes, both brought about by foolish action from Mr Bruce. The first occurred when he imported five hundred artisans from

(Above) The Malmsbury railway viaduct.
(Right) The western end of the railway tunnel at Elphinstone. Photo by John Henry Harvey.

Germany. His intention was to replace his workers with the immigrants at greatly reduced wages. The workers were angry and the potential for a huge dispute arose. The plan came badly unstuck and trouble was averted when the Germans sided with the workers already on the job and most of them moved off to other areas. Some stayed on, but at the ruling rate of fourteen shillings a day! No further action was called for by the workers.

The second, more serious, event came about when Bruce advised his workers, without notice, that paydays would be extended to once monthly instead of fortnightly. The men, especially those with families, lived from hand to mouth, and going a full month without any income presented them with a very difficult situation. They would almost certainly run out of food in the time between the last pay and the month to follow.

They lodged their strong objections with the company, to no avail. A strike was called, with many disruptive actions affecting work, and some ugly incidents took place. Work was effectively halted.

The crews at Taradale, Malmsbury and Big Hill angrily proclaimed support for their fellow workers and also went on strike. At Big Hill, the support was more direct and violent – carts making deliveries and pick-ups were stopped and turned around. A number of loaded carts were overturned and their drivers subjected to serious abuse,

An angry Mr Bruce declared: 'You gave me much injury and instead of drawing closer to me you widened the breach.'

He refused to give in, claiming that the government was at fault in being late with payments to him. This, he said, made it impossible for him to pay until he was paid by the government.

The issue was resolved when Bruce finally surrendered, on condition that the men returned to work immediately. They did.

✳ ✳ ✳

All along the line, work went on at a furious pace. It included the building of many bridges, culverts, drains, roads and viaducts. Almost every one of these structures is now heritage listed.

The viaduct at Malmsbury is a wonderful example of the skills of the time, the entire structure is held together by carefully placed keystones. It was built by Cornish and Bruce under the supervision of engineer George Darbyshire. It contains 38,000 cubic metres of bluestone, quarried a short distance to the east of the township and carried by horse and dray to the site. Work officially began on 25th October 1859. It was completed on 24th October 1860, an extraordinary achievement.

The *Mount Alexander Mail* of 26 October 1859 reported on the laying of the foundation stone. This honour went to the Commissioner of Public Works, Mr GWS Horne, before a gathering of over 500 people. As was the custom of the time, there were lengthy speeches from dignitaries, engineers, politicians and the like.

Mr ZEAL having returned thanks in suitable terms, a call was made for Dr McAdam, who expressed the hope that the works would be completed without accident. Mr Zeal having directed attention to the valuable assistance afforded by Mr Hull, and the compliment having been acknowledged by that gentleman, the invited guests adjourned to one of the workshops, in which a cold collation had been prepared. After justice had been done to the good things, Mr Zeal, who occupied the head of the table, proposed the health of the Queen, which was received with all the honours.

One speaker who held attention was Mr William Zeal of Castlemaine, a supervising engineer on this section. He was also the highly regarded MLA for Castlemaine in the Parliament. He is remembered by the Zeal Bridge on the road to Pennyweight Flat Cemetery. The sturdy masonry structure that bears his name replaced the timber bridge swept away in the devastating Castlemaine floods of 1889. Opened in 1890, it is heritage listed.[2]

Also among the several speakers that day was Mr William Bruce, principal of the contracting company. He revealed some astonishing figures associated with the railway works to that date: 'Between Malmsbury and Big Hill, hardly a square metre of ground had not been broken on up. We have moved 1,510,000 cubic yards of rock and earth; 276,640 cubic yards of ballast; 241,314 cubic feet of masonry; erected 125,670 yards of fencing; laid 77,400 yards of rail which weigh 15,480 tons.'[3]

---

2   Heritage listing: H69164.
3   Conversions:
    1,510,000 cubic yards of rock and earth = 1,145,00 cubic metres.
    276,640 cubic yards of ballast =211,500 m^3.
    241,314 cubic feet of masonry =184,497 m^3
    125670 yards of fencing =114,912 m.
    77,400 yards of rail = 70,000 m
    15,480 tons = 14,043 tonnes.

These figures are mind boggling. The viaduct has five spans of 18.3 metres and is 25 metres above the Coliban River. On the western approach, a culvert 35 metres long and ten metres wide was constructed, part of the Coliban water plan. Six hundred men worked on the Malmsbury section of the line alone, while a further 500 were employed in quarrying the bluestone for this and other projects which included sheds and housing.

The Taradale viaduct as it is now.

The population of Malmsbury grew rapidly from under 100 to around 1,000. A canvas town sprang up near the viaduct and accommodated hundreds of employees and some families. Sadly there was an outbreak of diphtheria causing the deaths of several children and adults.

The viaduct at Taradale is another engineering marvel of the time. It is one of Australia's most important railway structures; it is the oldest and largest of its kind in Australia. With a length of 60 metres of five spans of wrought iron box girders, this massive structure spans the valley of the Back Creek which runs through the centre of the township. Its highest point above the valley is 36 metres. The structure is supported by tiers of about 28,300 cubic metres of bluestone quarried from nearby Malmsbury. The structure contains some 1,370 tonnes of iron (by necessity imported from England), all held together by 310,000 rivets put in place by a team of 120 men.

The piers are sunk, on average, 16 metres below ground level, the northern abutment is 21 metres below ground level. By comparison the southern abutment is just 4 metres deep. The massive scaffolding contained about 1,700 cubic metres of timber. The planking on which the tracks were set was 100 millimetre thick red gum.

Other major structures on the railway to Bendigo were the impressive viaduct at Jackson's Creek (Sunbury) and the bridge at Riddell's Creek, but standing above all are the Taradale and Malmsbury viaducts and the tunnels at Elphinstone and Big Hill.

The line to Bendigo was officially opened for service on 20th October 1862. Work had been completed without serious incident at a cost of

£3,300,000. The extension to Echuca, a relatively easy task over flat land, was completed in 1864.

A small problem at Chewton caused some embarrassment. The line to the west of the railway station sloped downward so much that locomotives could not be stopped in time so that all the carriages would be alongside the platform. It was reported that the simple solution was to move the station slightly – good thinking! They did!

* * *

Considering the number of people employed on the line there were remarkably few fatalities.

At the Elphinstone tunnel, a man was walking on the nearly completed track when he was struck by a locomotive pulling a load of earth. The man's legs were severed. He was given prompt attention by Dr Robinson, but died at the scene.

At Kyneton, a worker fell beneath a train and was cut in half. In another tunnel incident, a man working in one of the three shafts was levering a large rock with a crowbar at the top level. He slipped and fell nineteen metres. The boulder weighing about 300 kilogram fell, crushing him. His body was taken to the nearby Four Mile Hotel for an autopsy.

Where do we build Castlemaine's station?

But the government had not finished with Castlemaine yet. It was yet to be decided where best to locate the railway station. The original plan was to place the station where it is today, adjacent to the eastern bank of Barkers Creek. However, there was a strong push to have it at the base of Clinkers Hill. The argument was that future development of the town would be to the south. Most of the reaction to this is lost in the mist of time, but 1,600 residents signed a memorial (petition) in support of the Barkers Creek site. This was sent to the head of the Railways Department.

On September 1860, the Municipal Council stated emphatically that Clinkers Hill was way off beam and the future was to the west. Winters Flat and the road to Muckleford was the way, Castlemaine being 'cramped for want of available land'. In the end, good sense prevailed and the station was built as originally planned. It has proved to be the ideal position. After

150 years, the council was finally proved to be correct – the west is now the way forward.

The railway has encouraged a lot of people to move from the crowded city to the quiet of Castlemaine. Many have brought their city ways and attitudes with them, which has upset some old-timers.

The railway is open for business

After considerable argument, the end of construction of the line to Sandhurst culminated in *two* grand opening ceremonies – one at Sandhurst and another at Castlemaine , five days apart. Surprisingly, on this occasion Castlemaine's celebrations were to come first!

From a newspaper report:[4]

> THE OPENING OF THE RAILWAY
> The opening of the line of railway to Castlemaine and Sandhurst having been definitely appointed for the 15th inst., a warm dispute has arisen between the two townships as to which shall do the honours of the occasion. The Municipal Councils of both places have been for some time engaged in negotiations, with, a view to effect a division of the festivities which are to mark the opening. Deputations from the Castlemaine Council have proceeded to Sandhurst, and the representative of the Sandhurst Council have visited Castlemaine, without, however, being able to agree as to terms. The Sandhurst Council proposed that a short lunch should be given at Castlemaine, and that the train should then proceed to Sandhurst, where a dinner and ball should take place, or that the train should run direct to Sandhurst, that the *dejeuner* should be given there and that the visitors should return, to partake of a dinner and ball at Castlemaine. Neither of these, suggestions, however, met with approval; and a third, that two days should be devoted to the celebration, one for each place was dismissed. Mr Mitchell determined that there should be two opening days, that Castlemaine's to take place and be

---

4   *Leader*, Sat 11 Oct 1862, p. 3.

celebrated upon the 15th inst., and that of Sandhurst upon the 20th. The preparations for the celebrations are being energetically proceeded with in both places.

On October 15th 1862, a most memorable day, three large locomotives huff and puff their way into the highly decorated Castlemaine railway station. This special train carries no less than the Governor, Sir Henry Barkley and his entourage. As well, the eight carriages are bursting with several hundred Melbourne dignitaries mingled with the common herd, all excited to be part of this massive event.

This day was Castlemaine's opportunity to put on an event; one that had never before been seen. And what an event it was!

The good people of Sandhurst didn't want to miss this show from what many considered the insignificant, unimaginative mob from lowly Castlemaine, so they put on a special train. No fewer than two hundred of them, including every dignitary from that proud town attended.

On alighting from his carriage, accompanied by his son, Sir Henry made an impromptu speech, surprising many when he promptly declared the line to Castlemaine and its new station open. Barkly and his group then entered the waiting barouche buggy, moving slowly toward the town. Great cheers and general applause followed as the good man passed through a guard of honour formed by 80 proud members of the Volunteer Castlemaine Rifles.

The *Mount Alexander Mail* reporter was ecstatic.

> 'Never before was there a scene of such excitement. The streets were adorned with tasteful, decorative, evergreens and flags. There were at least 7,000 people at the station when the train arrived from Melbourne. A carriage drawn by four fine white horses awaited the Governor.'

A procession moved through the decorated, archway-covered streets to the Castlemaine Hotel. The Governor and his party alighted, to the cheers of the large crowd, to rest prior to the afternoon banquet in the new Market Hall.

Oh, it was grand! Over 300 guests crammed into the banquet hall, the new market building, seated at tables laid across the width of the building.

At the centre of the head table were Sir Henry Barkly and his son. The meal was sumptuous, accompanied by a string of speeches, several lengthy enough to cure the most chronic insomniac.

Anybody who was anybody was there. Speechmakers included the Chief Secretary, MLAs, MLCs, local dignitaries such as Colonel Bull, William Bruce and railway engineers Smyth and Zeal, along with representatives of several local community organisations.

Eventually, the weary Governor and his entourage excused themselves and returned to the Castlemaine Hotel, to rest up for the Gala Ball. Dancing began at 9pm and continued until the early hours.

So ended a wonderful day of great excitement for Castlemaine and an event that must have caused the rival Sandhurst visitors to perhaps feel just a little unsure of their preparations for the 20th?

And now it's Sandhurst's turn

The Governor and his official party arrived mid-morning at Sandhurst railway station in a blast of whistles and steam. The assembled huge crowd went wild as the Governor stepped from the train where he promptly made a short speech, similar to that at Castlemaine five days before. The new line and new station, although far from completed, he declared open. There were more cheers of delight from thousands of throats.

The entire party was then transported through the streets, past more thousands of cheering citizens to their hotel to rest and prepare for what lay ahead – a special Sandhurst, country style lunch.

Sir Henry and his son were the guests at a huge banquet in the Town Hall where 800 guests enjoyed a massive four-course feast. As befits such an occasion there was again a lot of speech making and backslapping. At last, no doubt to his relief, the honoured guest and his group retired to their hotel for another spell.

But not for long! It was back on deck at 10.00pm for the Governor to be guest at the gigantic Town Hall ball. It seems half the town was there. Again, much food was consumed, along with copious quantities of liquid refreshment. By one o'clock in the morning, it was back to bed for the weary, speech-worn Governor.

Ah, what a night it was! The citizenry danced until 5.30am, when the exhausted musicians were finally allowed to throw in the towel. The weary revellers made their way to the station where the special train waited to take them back to the big city.

Alas, there was insufficient water and heat for the engine to raise enough steam to move. The dance- and booze-affected guests, thoroughly exhausted, were forced to wait until 12.30 pm before enough steam was produced for the locomotive to be moved. As a result, there were sleeping people to be seen on every seat and vacant doorway around the town.

Eventually all was in readiness for the cheer-filled departure. Travellers hung from every open window and doorway as the engine let go a mighty blast on the whistle. The train moved away as the assembled local crowd cheered themselves hoarse.

However, sparks from the engine set fire to the floral and gum leaf adorned timber archway over the railway line. This excellent and strikingly beautiful architectural decoration had been constructed by a group of volunteers for the occasion. A fierce fire ensued. The train

> CASTLEMAINE, 20TH OCTOBER.
> To-day has been observed as a holiday here, and several hundreds of people have gone to Sandhurst to witness the festivities.
> An engine, decorated with flags, etc., and driven by Mr. M'Carthy, left here with several carriages, carrying a great number of passengers and volunteers, also the bands of the Castlemaine and Chewton Rifles. There were great excitement and immense enthusiasm on arrival of Melbourne train here. Castlemaine people were surprised at the spirit of the Bendigo and Melbourne public.
> Several parties from Chewton and district who were not invited to the Castlemaine banquet, have accepted invitations from the Sandhurst Council, much to the annoyance and confusion of some of the Castlemaine officials.
> KYNETON, 20TH OCTOBER.
> This place has assumed quite a holiday appearance to-day, great numbers having left here to witness the formal opening of the railway to Sandhurst.

was quickly reversed from the growing inferno. The local fire brigade, with their hand-pulled fire wagon, was summoned, and, before long, the fire was out. Two hours later the train finally resumed the journey to Melbourne.

So ended a great day in the history of Sandhurst and the train service to Melbourne, so long dreamed of, became a reality.

PART FIVE

INDUSTRY AND OTHER THINGS

Mr Howe's Marked Tree

Just off Gaulton Street in Castlemaine, close to where Forest Creek and Barkers Creek converge with Campbells Creek, stands a giant River Red Gum tree. It is huge, about 27 metres tall, with a girth of six metres. It is estimated to be about 300 years old. Not many know of its existence and even fewer of its significant place in local history.

This magnificent example of *Eucalyptus camaldulensis* was marked as a point of reference by Government Surveyor William Weston Howe in 1842. It is shown on the 1854 map of Castlemaine town, marked clearly with an X and the notation 'the late Mr Howe's marked tree.'

Born and educated in England, Howe was a deputy to senior surveyor Robert Hoddle. In December 1842, Howe was upgraded to Town Surveyor at a council meeting held at the Royal Hotel in Collins Street, the Town Council's temporary meeting place The meeting had been called primarily to discuss the site for a new Town Hall. Howe was now on a hefty salary of two hundred and fifty pounds a year.[1]

---

1   Port Phillip Gazette, 4 Jan 1843, p. 2.

William Weston Howe's Marked Tree, junction of Barkers and Forest Creeks. Picture by the author, 2019..

Howe mapped much of the Loddon region and was charged with locating the headwaters of the Loddon River.

Unfortunately, he took ill and died whilst working at Mount Cole in 1849. Due to his attachment and considerable work in the area, he was buried at the tiny Franklinford Cemetery. His grave is clearly marked and tended with respect.

Mr Howe's Marked Tree is heritage listed and protected as an important landmark.

When Chewton was bigger than Melbourne!

The population of Chewton, the township that sprang up to serve the diggers of Forest Creek, has shrunk from 25,000 in 1852 to a mere 1300 today. But almost all of them are proud of the district's history and are fiercely parochial. Most of the buildings that lined Main Road have vanished, being replaced, of late, with homes that many say are totally inappropriate for a township so rich in heritage and history. Still remaining are several shopfronts; the Red Hill Hotel, complete with a disused music hall; remnants of a tiny bank building; the Town Hall and the Post Office.

But there has been a lot of change. A good example is the Red Hill pub. Now it is best described as a boutique hotel, dispensing craft beers and offering restaurant-style meals. It's a far cry from the days when rough-and-ready working men breasted the bar and quaffed large volumes of everyday beer. In those days, few women ever entered a pub and, when they did, it was to a separate room called the Ladies Lounge.

It is fair to say that the people are different, too. No longer are they the unkempt and uncouth workers from mines and foundries, or wood cutters, they are people who are a little more refined, certainly better educated, with jobs in offices or in retail.

The original name, Forest Creek, fell to the government's move to endow settlements with respectable British names, so Forest Creek became Chewton. To many it will always be Forest Creek, a township with a direct connection to its golden past. After all, it was the richest alluvial goldfield in the world, and its fame was known worldwide.

Bendigo has achieved the dream of its founders. It is now a thriving, prosperous metropolis of over 99,000 people, the fourth largest city in Victoria (Ballarat beats it by a whisker for third spot). Second place goes to Geelong with a population of nearly a quarter of a million. Melbourne has a population approaching five million.

The early vast stations, such as Barfold and Carlsruhe, are either non-existent or have been vastly reduced in size. The runs of thirty or fifty thousand acres are long gone. Many of the homesteads built by the prosperous owners remain. Some, like John Hepburn's Smeaton Hill, are magnificent and in excellent condition. Others are in decline. Glengower at Campbelltown, for example, owned now for many years by the Clarke family, has now been abandoned, even though it is a wonderful building. Its once busy shearing shed is long deserted and badly decaying, as are the huts and sheds. The cost of maintaining such grandeur is prohibitive for most current station owners. Across the road, the aged Black Duck hotel still operates.

Some Notable Industries

There have been some excellent and long-lasting industries established in Castlemaine over the years. Thompson's Foundry and the Castlemaine Bacon Company are two examples. Both are still flourishing businesses. Not so for the Castlemaine Woollen Mill established in 1875. The building was razed by fire and almost completely destroyed in 1981. It was probably struggling to survive at the time. The company battled on with reduced facilities and staff. A little over a decade later, what remained was severely damaged by another major fire. Again, the owners continued until it finally became unprofitable and was permanently shut down. But, for many years, it had been a highly successful, prosperous business and employed a large number.

One of the earliest attempts to establish an industry in the region came from William Hitchcock in 1856. He believed that there was a need for a flour mill and proposed one powered by steam, the latest method, to be built at Winter's Flat in Castlemaine.

A company was formed and six hundred shares were issued at ten pounds each. There was a disappointing result, with lukewarm interest in the project. Buyers were thin on the ground, but a substantial, well-equipped building soon rose on the site close to Forest Creek. Alas, not a single grain of wheat, or any other crop, was crushed by the plant before the company went into liquidation.

In December 1859, the building and plant was purchased by Cornish and Bruce to be converted into a foundry and machine shop to manufacture materials for the railway. A new heavy-draft chimney, necessary for heating furnaces, was the major alteration to the plant, and production began two months later. Having equipment and accessories produced close by was an asset to the railway worksite.

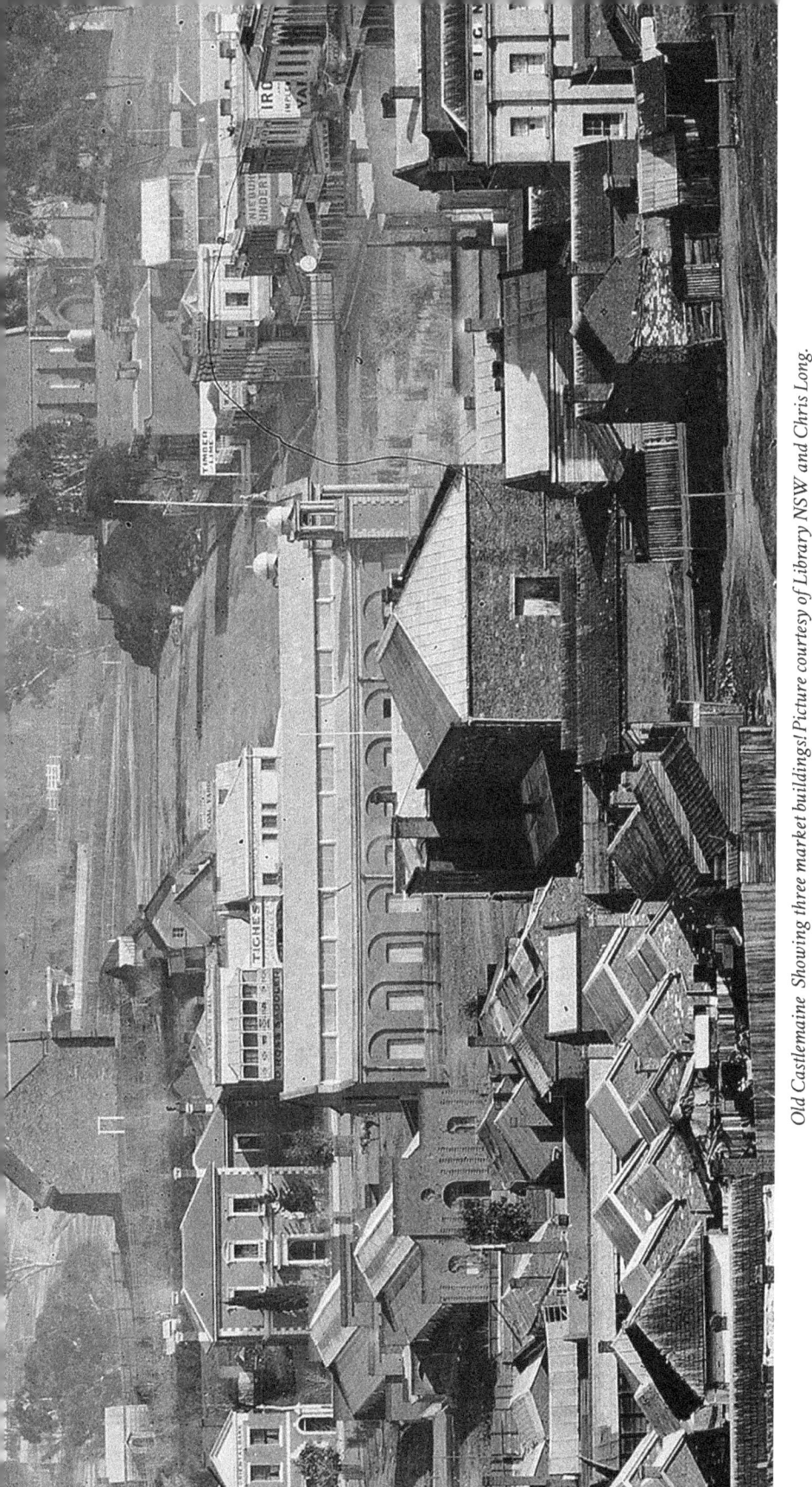

Old Castlemaine Showing three market buildings! Picture courtesy of Library NSW and Chris Long.

The remains of William Hitchcock's flour mill, 2019.

It was a time of considerable confidence in Castlemaine, which led to the Melbourne *Argus* newspaper getting a little carried away, describing Winter's Flat as a 'suburb of industry'.

In May of 1860, three months after the opening, Cornish and Bruce was forced to shut down temporarily. They had run into a serious problem with blacksmiths who had called a strike and downed tools in support of a claim for an eight hour working day. By the end of June, the company was forced to concede. This decision laid the foundation for a steady increase in successful claims and placed Australia as a leader in reduced working hours for all.

The foundry building was demolished in 1979, but the original flour mill remains intact, although it is not considered safe to enter. Two features of the old mill were its gigantic chimney stack and the large clock that faced the town. It

An old landmark disappears, the demoliton of the Cornish and Bruce Chimney.
Bendigonian *11 Oct 1917.*

kept time for the people of Castlemaine for many years until that section of the mill was demolished. On the site rose Cusack's Garage which was the first drive-in American style petrol/service station in Australia. It is now a car tyre and auto service.

Thompsons Foundry

There were three major foundries in the region in the 19th century, all in Castlemaine. Apart from Cornish and Bruce, already mentioned, there were Vivians, and Thompsons. The latter has been the only survivor, functioning successfully since 1875, although now known as Flowserve and under foreign ownership. Originally it was a flour mill set up in 1864 by two brothers David and James Thompson. Part of the original building is included in the modern-day offices of the present company.

Not long out from Ireland the brothers set up a partnership and erected a very successful and prosperous quartz crushing plant on Quartz Hill in the Castlemaine district. For the next decade, they worked at all sorts of offshoots from that – erecting equipment for the mines: engines, pumps, winding gear and so forth. Seeing a need, they then moved into flour milling in 1864, hence the mill in Parker Street, Castlemaine. They gained a number of prizes for their flour, including an award for quality at the 1867 Paris Exhibition. In 1875, the Thompsons began taking engineering work at the premises, and two years later, milling was abandoned in favour of engineering. The works rapidly expanded and by 1887 employed more than 120 men. One of their earliest contracts was for the supply of switching points and crossings for the Victorian Railways, a contract still held over a century later, though now fulfilled by Vossloh Cogifer who bought out Thompson, Kelly and Lewis in about 2008. The company also built steam powered locomotives and other steam powered vehicles and equipment such as steamrollers and ships' engines. By 1919, Thompsons had built sixty locomotives for the Victorian Railways and an additional twenty-one for the Commonwealth.

Among its many important manufacturing achievements are major works for the Snowy

Locomotive builders plate. Thompsons Foundry, 1914.

Hydro Scheme, the supply of towers for the West Gate Bridge and the construction of the old Williamstown ferry. This ferry connected Williamstown to Port Melbourne for many years prior to the opening of the West Gate Bridge. As well as the head office and foundry in Castlemaine, the company once operated a branch factory on the waterfront in Williamstown.

During both world wars, Thompsons provided valuable equipment for warfare. Thompsons Foundry has also trained innumerable people in the various skills associated with engineering work, thus making a valuable contribution to the nation. Many current Castlemaine residents owe their careers to the excellent training they received at what is commonly called 'The Foundry'. The business today is focused primarily on assembling valves and pumps of all sizes and descriptions and is quite successful.

David Thompson, the company's founder, died in 1888. The business passed into full control of David Junior when his brother James retired later that same year. David jnr's interests extended to music, and he was a founding member and President of Thompson's Foundry Band, which is still a well-loved local institution.

Thompsons Foundry (now Flowserve) in 2019.
Some of the original bulding is still used as part of the offices.

He continued in the band until his unfortunate death on 16th February 1916. With his foreman James Miller, he was standing beside a locomotive that was under construction. The overheard crane struck a part of the engine's boiler causing the locomotive to tip over. It fell on the men who both died from their injuries.

Although the foundry is but a shadow of the 700 or so it once employed, it remains an important industry for the region.

Vivian's Foundry.

Although it was a large and flourishing business, Vivian's Foundry remains a bit of a mystery. Not a lot of detail can be found in our usual sources. We know that the founders were George Vivian and his brother Charles, immigrants from Wales. The pair were no doubt attracted by the opportunities they saw on the goldfield. We do not know if they were successful in their search for gold, but we know they began foundry type work, probably about 1855, at their property on Moonlight Flat on the eastern edge of Castlemaine.

An item in the *Argus* announced that they had completed work on building a foundry in Mostyn Street, Castlemaine. The article said: 'A very great want is supplied by Vivian and Co.' This seems to indicate that it was the first foundry in the area. What has been termed the Pay Cottage still stands at 104 Mostyn Street, as do large sections of the foundry's stone walls.

> *A Foundry.*—We are glad to be able to state that a very great want in this district is supplied by Messrs. Vivian & Co., who have just completed the erection of a foundry, where all kinds of brass and iron founding may be executed speedily. This establishment will prove an immense convenience to the machine proprietors in Castlemaine, Tarrangower, Fryer's Creek, and adjacent localities. Hitherto damages to machinery had frequently to be repaired in Melbourne, causing great loss by delay. In two cases which occurred lately, the working of machines were suspended for six weeks, owing to the necessity for sending to town for repairs of injuries, and not a week passes without the occurrence of a similar instance. Messrs. Vivian's establishment will enable machiners to avoid this delay, and will no doubt be well supported.

Argus, 9th May 1857.

Not long after the commencement of the business, George Vivian built a substantial new home at the top of Mostyn Street, number 167, now heritage listed. The home is in a prime location, overlooking the town, with the remnants of Vivian's Foundry a stone's throw below. No doubt George gained much satisfaction from looking down on the great business that he and his brother had created. Among his many achievements, George invented and patented a hydraulic jack hammer which was widely used in mining activities across the land. George appeared to be the driving force, as his brother is not prominently mentioned. George suffered a stroke early on and he travelled to England in an effort to find a cure. It was not a success and he soon came home. He sold the business within a few years.

George Vivian headstone, Castlemaine Cemetery.

Over time, much of the foundry equipment is believed to have found its way to Thompson's Foundry.

George died in 1886. His grave is in the Castlemaine cemetery, marked by an imposing headstone. We are indebted to George Vivian's grandson, Chris Long, and historian James Taylor for supplying this information.

Images to the right:
1. *Vivians Foundry*
2. *Vvivians Foundry. Part of the stone wall remains and the building bearing the sign Castlemaine Foundry remains intact.*
3. *Another view of Vivians Foundry*
4. *Vivians mining eqiupment on an abandoned mine site, Tibooburra in far west NSW.*

Very early Castlemaine. Note the clock on the Cornish & Bruce foundry and the poppet head in the background (far left). Picture from the Library of NSW, courtesy of Chris Long.

George Weston Foods factory at Castlemaine in 2019. Originally Harris' Castlemaine Bacon Co..

Castlemaine Bacon Company

Although it did not begin in the early days of white settlement, no story of the district's industry would be complete without mention of the Castlemaine Bacon Company.

In 1905, two young men, Wright Harris and John Weetman, who had become friends when living at Scoresby, moved to Castlemaine. Their intention was to establish a bacon factory to serve the population of the small town. Wright was the son of English migrants and had no experience in the butchering trade. However, John had served an apprenticeship in the highly specialised trade of pork butchering in Sheffield, England. As well as general butchering, he learned from experts how to make quality smallgoods.

In 1882, he headed for Australia to set up a new life, leaving his wife and child in England. He worked his trade in Gippsland for five years before returning to his home town to bring his family to Australia.

The two friends moved to Castlemaine where they purchased the bacon section of the Maine Butter Company in Kennedy Street. They had opposition in the town from another smallgoods maker, Julius Khule.

Engaging the help of a mutual friend, the company began work initially processing five pigs per week. The business grew and soon it was necessary to move to larger premises in Richards Road.[2]

The Castlemaine Bacon Company grew to the point of processing not five pigs a week, but five thousand by 1977, with the capacity to move 1700 a day. Ultimately, sales and distribution centres were required across Australia. Today the company employs up to 1200 people.

In 2003 the company merged with Chinese smallgoods maker Dennis Jen who acquired full ownership in 2005. The Harris family connection ended. Since then the factory has grown even more and now occupies a large part of Odger's Road to the north-west of Castlemaine. The company has two large piggeries at Bears Lagoon and another at Girgarre, some distance to the north. Ownership is now in the hands of multinational George Weston foods.

Their famous slogan is 'Is Don is Good' and it *is* true that Don is good … good for Castlemaine.

---

[2] The complete Harris Family story is told in *Bringing home the Bacon* by Leigh Edmunds, published by Monash, and the authors acknowledge that as the source of this information. It is a remarkable success story.

EPILOGUE

BIG CHANGES COME TO TOWN

There is so much to write about concerning the land we love that it cannot possibly be done in any single publication. There has been huge progress and change since Major Thomas Mitchell and his team passed through in 1836. The land as it is today would be unimaginable to them.

Although the changes are enormous, much of the landscape remains easily recognisable. For example, what were once clear-flowing streams are now waterways clogged with weed and scrubby growth – much of it imported weeds such as blackberry and gorse. The white people have polluted them and even changed their courses. Examples of both are Forest Creek and Barkers Creek.

The dual railway tracks linking Melbourne to the Murray, established in the 1850s and 1860s, have been replaced by a single track controlled by modern electronic wizardry. Modern fast trains run in each direction almost half hourly for much of each day.

This progressive change has encouraged people from the increasingly crowded city of Melbourne to move to regional towns such as Kyneton and Castlemaine. Both of these towns have gone through serious, dramatic changes. The streetscapes remain much as they were a century ago, but the businesses that operate in them are vastly different. Individual small

Forest Creek, as it is today.

stores have given way to supermarkets, cafes, art galleries, coffee and antique shops.

Different also are many of the people who occupy the homes, with a large number of city people choosing life in the country.

There are two obvious reasons, apart from the attraction of quiet living: the excellent train service offers fast transfer to jobs in the city, and more achievable house prices. Many people struggling with their city mortgage have sold their Northcote, Fitzroy or similar suburban homes for maybe a million dollars. Similar homes in Kyneton or Castlemaine are, or were, half of that. The benefit is pretty easy to see.

Prices have risen steadily in both towns, but remain much more within the budgets of the better employed and educated that appear to make up the bulk of 'tree changers'. In a good number of instances, such people have been able to buy a home and have substantial amounts of cash left over. Both towns can probably be described as 'dormitory towns', where many breadwinners are absent in daylight hours on weekdays and resident on weekends.

That's the end of it

www.ingramcontent.com/pod-product-compliance
Lightning Source LLC
Chambersburg PA
CBHW051548010526
44118CB00022B/2623